ALISE SPINELLA, *MEDITATION DRAWING DAY TWENTY FIVE*, 2014, ACRYLIC, INK, COLORED PENCIL, GRAPHITE ON PAPER, 30 X 22 INCHES. PHOTO: JOSHUA WHITE

LOS ANGELES REVIEW OF BOOKS QUARTERLY JOURNAL | FALL 2016

COVER ART
THOMAS LAWSON, FRONT COVER: *THE HANGED MAN*, 2011, OIL ON CANVAS, 72 X 60 INCHES.
BACK COVER: *THE NEW WORLD: TWINS, 2008, OIL ON CANVAS, 72 X 60 INCHES. PHOTO: FREDRIK NILSEN.*
COURTESY OF DAVID KORDANSKY GALLERY, LOS ANGELES, CA.

The Los Angeles Review of Books is a 501(c)(3) nonprofit organization. The *LARB Quarterly Journal* is published quarterly by the Los Angeles Review of Books, 6671 Sunset Blvd., Suite 1521, Los Angeles, CA 90028. Submissions for the *Journal* can be emailed to EDITORIAL@LAREVIEWOFBOOKS.ORG. Visit our website at WWW.LAREVIEWOFBOOKS.ORG.

The *LARB Quarterly Journal* is a premium of the LARB Membership Program. Annual subscriptions are available. Go to WWW.LAREVIEWOFBOOKS.ORG/MEMBERSHIP for more information or email MEMBERSHIP@LAREVIEWOFBOOKS.ORG.

Distribution through Publishers Group West. If you are a retailer and would like to order the *LARB Quarterly Journal*, call 800-788-3123 or email orderentry@perseusbooks.com.

To place an ad in the *LARB Quarterly Journal*, email ADSALES@LAREVIEWOFBOOKS.ORG.

CONTENTS
FALL 2016

FICTION

POETRY

FEATURES

FROM THE EDITOR

The theme of the issue you hold in your hands is a natural fit for LARB: writing from Los Angeles. Over the past five years we have worked hard to demonstrate to the rest of the world what many of us have known all along – that Los Angeles is a city of groundbreaking artists in every genre, and of voracious, open-minded consumers of culture. We are, in short, a cultural capital. In 2016 our mission was aided by a generous grant from the Goldhirsh Foundation's LA2050 initiative, which enabled us to feature a piece by or about an LA-based creative on our website every single day. The fact that we never lacked for material testifies to the vibrancy of our cultural landscape. We are capping the year off with an issue of the Literary Quarterly that reflects some of the great variety of work being done in our city. In this issue we have placed special emphasis on emerging voices from a wide range of backgrounds. Let LARB and Los Angeles stand as models of openness and inclusiveness as we head into 2017.

– Boris Dralyuk, Executive Editor

KARLEY SULLIVAN, *UNTITLED MICRO I*, 2016, ARCHIVAL PIGMENT PRINT, DIMENSIONS VARIABLE

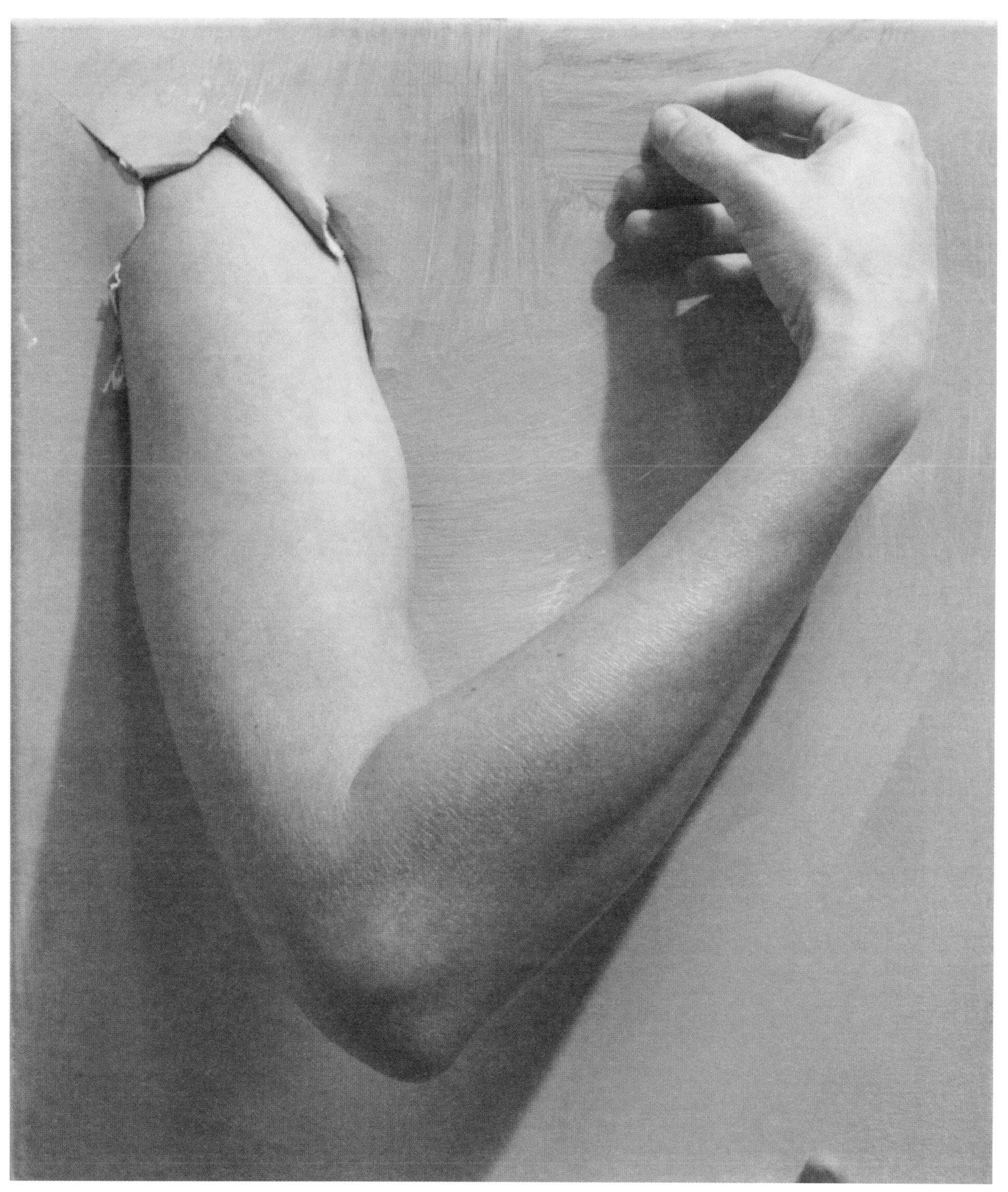

SARAH SARCHIN, *BARE ARM*, 2014, INKJET PRINT, 13 X 11 INCHES.

SARAH SARCHIN, *PICASSO*, 2016, OIL ON LINEN, 16 X 20 INCHES.

PERSISTENCE IN PRACTICE

JEN GEORGE

IN AN EFFORT to trump time or at least use it, or else as something absorbent to shore up the leaks of identity or existence that had sprung due to time, I had undertaken work I hoped to be of value after looking at selected and collected paintings of multiple people in sexual situations that were being displayed at galleries and museums citywide in a campaign the Los Angeles Arts Board called Coming at Once, which was heavily advertised via banner, billboard, newspaper, and TV commercials. I set about my undertaking with variations on the same approach; clenched hands and menstruating (or something like it) often, I would gain experience. I spent days, at first, and then that turned into years, attempting to develop a mark or a signature, the results of which looked crude but possibly distinct. With the morning sun I would make a spiked tea and vomit so as to employ bulimia as a practice of devotion to something that would one day show itself to me: the purpose. I forgot both the cause and the genesis during this trajectory and became ill. I sought cures and purchased remedial products with my credit card. The nights were all the same. At each sunset, I'd reflect with a koan found in my employer's Advanced Brand Philosophies handbook: *what was that all about*. I often felt as if I'd watched a long Eastern European film I didn't understand. I'd sleep like a log, only waking up to give sleep blowjobs once or twice each night, performed on various people who I'd wanted to critique or contextualize my art. In the morning, I'd set about straining the tea, vomit, say prayers for no appetite, and watch the daily parades on television. Certain practices persist. I keep many traditions from the illness, and continue with my work daily, indirectly, and in hopes.

¤

The float makers always topped themselves, innovating wildly or not at all in turns, using only flowers attached to mesh molds as material. In the parade archives shown on the rerun channel, one can see that the floats used to be simpler in nature; only zoo or domestic animals and sometimes horses, recalling the area's less settled days, with obvious choices like black-eyed-Susans for something like pack mule eyes. The float subject matter has evolved, like all things, according to the fashions; the current motifs reference the recently past, and possibly still present, golden age of large malls and advertisements. The float designers are celebrated only briefly; one day you are the greatest float maker with your vision, the next you are living in your float as it rots at the end of the parade route, despite your religious use of flower freshener, aspirin, and pennies, having abandoned your loved ones for your vision.

When I turn off the TV each day I think maybe I'll go in person to the parade. Because of the procession's early hour, I've never made it. The state is going broke paying for the flower business in both water and cold hard cash, and there are op-ed arguments in the papers suggesting economic resolutions, along with daily thematic and individual criticism of the floats. But, everyone loves the floats in perpetuity, including even the most critical op-eds.

Some days there is a distinct feeling that is echoed in people shopping in stores and on the streets, or else the sidewalks of the promenades and plazas and strip malls. It's best communicated as a thought, as no one speaks the words in the exact manner of the energy, which is: Prince Charmant lives here! I'm up for anything! That's just me in a nutshell if that makes sense!

I discuss my work when asked, anticipating that my words will generate something material. "I'm looking to do some paint jabs and smears. Maybe abstract in the older way of queer New Mexican hermits. Newer ideologies are more me, but with firm roots in what has come before so as to have ground upon which to stand," I say, leaving room for someone to fill in the blanks. No one does. My language regarding answers about my work, or else delivery of the language, has some mistaken, thinking I am something like their Prince Charmant in terms of cultural or social agency.

At a party, people are smoking real cigarettes again. I remember that from the last beginnings of the consumer cycle, which was heralded in by a sweeping devil-may-care attitude regarding health and money spent on clothing, and is now seeing a revival, but with health foods and supplements to counteract negative consequences. There are discussions of who is good artistically and who is not, and the ways what's good can be reduced to formula, and the ways the people accusing others of being formulaic suggest their own work and ideas are impervious to becoming formulaic and are therefore better than what is being called good.

"Where should we move now?" says a member of a group of people who refer to each other as "us" and are all trying to believe, both ambiguously and ambitiously, in the exact same thing.

"There's that new living room on the outer edge of the valley that has couches inside and outside. We can smoke there," a performance artist who works at a museum customer service desk suggests.

"We've heard of it!" they say.

Everyone drives to the living room with the backyard and we pay to get in.

I'm not hungry because of the Ephedrine I take, but the living room has little tables with packages of health crackers. The key with Ephedrine use is hydration, and so I drink water from a mini fridge. The discussion is on monogamy porn, where married couples are required to sleep with other people for their jobs as sex workers, but maintain a deep, abiding, and true love for each other.

"It's heartfelt," a crate builder explains.

"The story is good because it's a love story," says someone else who works at the crate-making place.

"I don't get it," I say.

"They have to have sex with other people," the crating company owner explains, "but that's not their main thing. Their main thing is having a nice family and a good life."

"That's what people want?" I say.

"Yes," more than one person answers. The topic of conversation among the group turns to criminal Olympians — Olympians convicted of crimes after glory, rather than sportspeople whose skill is criminally good. Someone suggests floats should be made of the criminal Olympians. With little interest in Olympians beyond performance during their games, and thinking that float theme idea would be unsuccessful, I take a load off on the plastic chair in the backyard. The wind whips from the Santa Anas and aerates my outer menstrual area. The wet metallic odor lingers and is becoming something of its own signature.

In the morning I vomit with the sun. Still, the purpose is unclear, but my anxiety, libido, and ambition are unceasing, like the night blowjobs. I receive my special milks and juice delivery and drink them. They are free of most things and what's added is purely multi-leveled. I stand upon the balcony, my materials strewn. The palm trees tell of the strong wind — the rows or clusters of them never end, and the tops may come off at some point. I squeeze large quantities of paint onto a flattened refrigerator box. The wind lifts and levitates the oversized palette briefly before carrying it off.

At another party with food I do not eat because I am trying, really, to be free of things, and because I have been told by an art agent who (kindly) offered the free advice that I am too poor to look as curvy as I do, someone who is known for their ideas says outright, "Hey I'm Prince Charmant, what are you working on?"

"Several things," I tell him, "in three dimensions as far as materials, or more if you count intent and failure with a persistent desire for success or vision as dimensions."

"There's so much art here now!" a woman who overhears our conversation says.

"And in terms of the landscape it's so nice how the mountains crash into the ocean and how the ground is always moving," I say. The woman who interrupted me and the man with ideas go off together. I stand by myself for some time. Before leaving, the art agent circles back, giving me the address for a big house where people have biweekly group sex in a large, carpeted den. "It's very current and in accordance with the city's art campaign," he tells me. "It'd be good for someone like you."

At my balcony studio, my gums begin to bleed. All of my pillows have brown stains, as well as the upper part of my sheets, and a brownish ring on the man's penis from night blowjobs. Since the winds have taken many of my lighter materials — papers, pens, oil crayons, brushes, and notebooks — I note that I need heavier things. The sunsets have been exactly the same every night.

I go to work at the liquid supplement shop located on a long street in the Beverly Center II, more eastern than the first. The employees are all solid or rotund or buxom, some could be called strong, hired so that the proprietors do not seem discriminatory toward a healthy look of which I'm in possession and trying to rid myself of. I don't apologize for my shape to the customers who want either promises of being smaller or else possession of someone small, as a matter of pretended or performed pride in self, but at the same time I keep up with the attempted bulimia, which is private, and totally against the company-brand philosophy, which is something like self-acceptance and personal greatness and superiority. There have been several handbooks written on what the company does and does not believe, the attitudes within changing with the fashions, outdated beliefs erased by the burning of the passé handbooks. At orientation we were told, repeatedly, "Our customer is special because they have a lot of money to spend and would like to be healthier and more attractive and live longer than other people and feel great while doing it. Our customer will escape trappings via currency, which is what our product provides." We were told to genuinely flatter our customers, sexually and sartorially, or however else they might want. For example, some women wanted to be someone else, some men wanted to be themselves, so we'd improvise. As employees, our eyes and skin glow because we take the supplements offered at our shop, all of which are luminous and tightening in effect, though we're only supposed to have one a day. We steal the products, the company steals our time, and anyway for what we (as employees) do to be considered stealing, we'd have to believe in the capitalist law of private property, which, as employees, we do not. We get paid so minimally that as a group we've discussed joining the Socialist Party of Los Angeles, though we're unsure if there is one. No one has looked it up, and we're all a little more comfortable stealing from the company than starting a revolution. "Opiating the corporate octopus so when it comes time we can sever the tentacles," we half joke. Sometimes I cry when thinking about severing actual octopus tentacles. We take breaks in the back and roll our eyes when customers come in and answer them minimally because it's how we're paid and we'd like them to get lost, though it's against company policy to act this way outright. I drink a brown potion; this one is expensive, but not even the most. To a new customer I say, "My mother loves this one!" regarding a product old women who would like to look younger buy that she has picked up. She leaves. To the next customer interested in the same product I say, "My mother's wrinkles disappeared and she even moved out of her basement apartment in the Valley after the cumulative effects of all of our products combined and she's so much stronger now — like lifts weights and has graduated to the next level in her weightlifting class. Her neck got thick but it looks like a thousand dollars on her, which is, incidentally, the price of this supplement, and also my monthly income and the cost of my balcony studio rent." We do get a small commission in the form of employee of the month stickers so I try sometimes. I take another break and ride the Bev Center II's steep escalator. I drink a non-glycemic, pearl-like potion that does have pearls in it. At closing my co-workers and I hang up our aprons, say rude comments about the customers, and tell each other we'll see each other again next shift.

I receive my next shipment of powders, pulses, and juices and, coupled with my libido enhancers, I walk through the farmers markets of greater Los Angeles with great speed, sweating. Returning to my balcony studio without purchases due to insufficient funds, I look out over some private backyards where dogs sit in the shade and cats sit in the sun. The height of the building, low but high enough, gives me this view, not that I'm on an affluent hill with mountainous or oceanic views. The man stirs in the balcony bed. "It was too quiet," he says. That's why he slept so long — days, maybe longer, though I'd been out so often I couldn't speak to how much or little he actually slept. "I went to the farmers market," I tell him. "My libido was raging from the tonics, milks, and enhancers. It was fun!" He is not really awake. "I sampled three different baked goods, then threw them up in a trashcan by the petting zoo since they were not free of anything. Then I pet a chick and a baby goat. The goat was like a little devil — actually satanic, and I was afraid he was going to step on the chick, or else ram her with his little horns. Do goats eat chickens?"

"No."

"This one might," I say. I take out some trays with crusted paint and a jar of turpentine and mix the two around.

"What about this technique?" I ask him, mixing. He smokes and shrugs. "I think I'm getting at something," I say.

"It's possible that gross misuse of and clumsiness with materials and methods may be what follows de-skilling," he says.

I find the big house easily via bus and a long walk. In the kitchen, I say to the group of people, "Here for the orgy?" unsure if they are or not. They laugh because saying what is true and plain makes people laugh, but the genesis of the laughter is automatic — like my work theft — or else a disguise for something we cannot say. Momentarily, I think I have come to the wrong place. Then the men are offered Dewar's.

"Oh good!" they say, and drink heavily.

The women are offered after, both Dewar's and as sex objects since the group's focus, instead of ousting the accepted tradition of women as sex objects, is for women to embrace and enjoy objectification. We all act as appropriately as possible. Some people try to make other jokes in imitation of mine the drunker we get, saying, "Wait, is this going to be an orgy?" but it doesn't have the same effect or automatic response as my joke. Others get quietly angry or distracted or disappointed or internal or full of self-doubt, and it's looking like the evening's formation is taking shape. Everyone is horny and insecure enough that action can begin, led by the woman of the house at her disrobing. It's hard to tell the shape of the physical arrangement once things are going. Those who are not physically adept are especially not so in intimate settings no matter the number, and clumsiness really shows itself. There are two such people whose rhythm is off entirely and we all have to pretend like they aren't or like we don't notice it, or like what they are doing feels good when in fact it's like an unskilled line cook hammering chicken to make chicken paillard. Some are enjoying themselves in earnest; there are many genuine faces being made. My menstrual blood is pink and therefore fairly Charmant to many. When the action concludes, or most have stopped, the woman of the house goes to take a load off in the bathroom for some time wherein she looks at her personal pornos on her device (bigger than everyone's because she is a homeowner) and sends us personal messages reviewing individual performance as we sit in the living room looking at pornos on our little ones. The orgies in the pornos we watch look different than what has just taken place. I receive a personal message from the woman of the house: you're wilder than I would have thought, but aimless and clearly trying to map overall meaning during action, which is off-putting to me since I'm the one orchestrating and hosting this thing and would like all participants to be lost in the moment totally. I'm grateful for the feedback, but uncertain I can do better. I try to look on other people's devices to see what their feedback is, but nothing is well defined.

Again the night and recalling the situations of the day, I practice the ABP koan: what was that all about.

After a string of uninspired floats the tenor of the op-eds grows impatient and then violent. They can't all be great! Says one, excusing the subpar themes and executions after a future-in-technology motif has gone on too long. We demand better, though God knows we don't deserve it, says another who was known for his high standards, extreme self-loathing, and belief in God. Why are the floats ongoing? The pageantry and celebration are not only a distraction from reality, but unsustainable on a daily level and also long-term, as well as the city paying poverty wages to maintenance, security, and clean-up workers, says an ed who was sensible but a downer and seriously not in accord with the ethos of the city at all. I can make floats that are better and will take us to another level, artistically and on the whole, and beyond, but no one will look at my plans or even my written proposal, and I'm considering taking serious violent action in the form of an enormous, high-powered hose directed at the floats on the parade route, another, whose op-eds were almost never read, writes.

I channel numerous energies for my work from my balcony studio; today there are a lot of legacies or old people wishing they had them. The energy drifts through the city like the palm fronds that are always whipping about at my face and legs, only psychically rather than physically painful. The city is filled with old people in manors and estates with only grown children, without children of their own. When alone, instead of disgusting faces, they make lonely wishes for more of themselves to leave behind: skid marks (in the spirit of bathroom humor, as one energy I pick up on suggests), otherwise their wishes come in the form of names on theater chairs or museum benches or sidewalk plaques: little tombstones in the larger graveyard of the city (in the spirit of bad metaphors, as another energy demands). On the balcony, hesitant and irresolute, I set about action in the energy people do when embarking without destination repeatedly. I mix the paint colors in multiple tubs until they are gray-brown. All the old symptoms from the morning crop up, added onto that — a feeling of unreality due to the particular combination of supplements, tea, and Ephedrine. It's fine. I have been menstruating (or something like it) for, possibly, months. It could be hormones. Or polyps. Large fibroids. Uterine cancer. To rinse off I use the balcony hose, which comes in handy for hygiene and thirst, but not the small turpentine rag fires that flare up on occasion. I look to the television and see the flower-parade countdown clock. It's something to look forward to. Upon the balcony, I tie a noose and throw it over the side, the loop so heavy in the rope style it takes with it my balcony chair down to the sidewalk, which is always empty.

A sunset: It never ends.

To the palm trees: Get a life.

At the supplement shop I flirt in a brazen manner with a handsome man I think to be rich or in possession of the means necessary to change my life. I pour his liquid supplement (a silver milk tonic that is our most expensive) to suggest a coming penis, dip my finger in and lick it, to suggest me licking his penis or his semen, give my finger a little blowjob, to suggest giving a blowjob, do some little dance while ringing him up where I rub my butt (outside the jeans), to display a sex simulation and moves I like doing during those types of encounters. He pays and puts a long joint in the tip jar. I immediately take the joint out of the tip jar and put it in my apron pocket. The man asks for my information.

"I can take you places. I have a car," he says.

"I love being driven around," I say.

In bed, wind whipping my hair, I reflect on the day with the ABP koan: what was that all about.

Because of the relative success of my last joke at the big house, I consider the possibility of comedy. I conceive of another joke for our situation — stylistically more improv than stand-up. After the action of the group begins, I yell out, "Don't touch me!" and though no one is (yet), everyone backs away. I begin to explain the joke, knowing not to take it too far since timing is everything in comedy (as in finance, as my father used to say).

"It's a joke because we're all clearly in agreement!" I explain. But people are upset. "I'm sorry," I say. "It's just not funny," a woman with nice breasts who smokes the long joint tells me. She is forgiving, and tonight I like her best, though it's somewhat against group policy for women of the group to like anyone, especially another woman, best.

After everything, the woman of the house sends me a personal message: No more jokes, okay? Also, refer to last critique.

The new parade is on after the night. The teaser float is a dragon, and is both longer and wider than the Beverly Center of days past. The dragon speaks nothing of our cultural atmosphere in which there is nothing mythical or strong — with its long tail, red and gold chrysanthemums, the dragon is something other than us. The Bev Center from days past was so much more in keeping with the city's trademark philosophy, and most op-eds agree all floats should be a reflection. The following float is a mountain just as big and in the likeness of Baldy, made of blue-green hydrangeas. "They're getting so sentimental and wannabe romantic. It's our entire age and personally I'm sick of it," I say to the man on my balcony studio, a straggler from the big house that possibly gave me a ride home. I'm thinking of writing an op-ed and trying various positions out in hopes a strong one will influence my work or make me known to others. "But then too I was sick of the age in which all ideas were concealed and shrouded and elaborately wrapped up or laboriously masked so you didn't know what anyone's intentions were at all — eventually, everyone caught on that there are only so many motions and ideas and concepts and fantasies, and got fed up and were just like, out with it already."

The man in the balcony studio likes when I speak this way, calling our conversation a discourse on persistent matters of the day. "A discourse on persistent matters of the day!" he says. "Which brings us to our current age!" He licks his lips, possibly thinking of an op-ed himself. This is foreplay for the man, who is not tired after the night at the big house, or the night blowjobs, or our menstrual (or polyp or fibroid or uterine cancer) sex. He doesn't mind my mouth bleeding or the rings on his penis like the last man (who didn't say anything directly but made certain faces) did. "We analyze everything before it even happens, or immediately after it ended!" He drinks my juices and swallows my libido enhancers. "And then you have the museums sitting on their high horses and lording over the elitist parts of the city with an education in the classics leading to the museum visitors attempting to memorize the names of all those stupid fucking busts populating their never-ending halls!" he says, naked, crusted blood all over, and sipping the spiked tea that has been brewing in the sun for days. The man hates busts, especially the one I'm working on, which will be Gene Autry once I can get past the block form.

"Why him?" The man at my studio asks, talking about Gene.

"It's just who I think is hiding in this block," I tell him, taking a chisel to the big rock.

There is an announcement in the paper saying, Here's Your Art, L.A.! I don't read the entire thing, but it's something about the new museums and wings. The current man in the studio, an art handler, having seen the announcement also, has an opinion because he has a general interest in institutional matters, failures, and dissections thereof.

"The museum employees quit because of the frequency of changing hands," he says diagnostically. "And then there was the matter of the triple show of a board member that left lots of non-aficionados and amateurs like myself thinking: why does she get that?"

"I looked at the paintings of that board member and kind of loved them," I say, remembering a visit to the galleries when I worked there and got free tickets. The new wing of the museum had employed aspiring artists to stand outside and say, WE'RE NOT OPEN YET CAN YOU EVEN NAME FIVE ARTISTS IN THE MUSEUM DO YOU EVEN HAVE TICKETS THEY'RE REQUIRED AND HARD TO GET, upon opening to generate feelings of both exclusion and exclusivity among the patrons. The museum had hired an artist, well known for both his voyeuristic fetishes and creating situations of unease and then watching and recording himself masturbating from a control room as the situations turned chaotic, to write the lines and direct the employees. Heat lamps in the already hot weather made conditions punishing and tense for both employees and patrons. I thought I had been good at delivering the lines, but was fired after two weeks because it was rumored the artist got tired of the same player's (employee's) responses to the situations. The spiked tea does not make my visitor vomit.

"Since this is a studio visit," I say, pouring more tea, "What I'd like is an assessment of my work." He looks at my things on the balcony. "Not so much imitative as easily impressionable, which isn't worse, but not better either," he says.

In the paper I read the last op-ed in a series about the city officially defining itself in concrete terms: something else about the city is the elderly are employed by grocery stores. It's cute! It makes everything slow. It takes forever in the cashier's line, and for the old people to collect the carts, so that lines are long and carts are limited. The same for pizza delivery persons — all geriatric, and pizza takes so long they've had to change to a two-hours-or-less policy. Since I've noticed it, one can only conclude that it is at least one, if not the only, identifying feature of our city.

Someone brings a two pounder of chocolates to the supplement shop despite the rule that we're not supposed to eat any sugar on the job because of cancer, anger, and red complexions, and my bulimia hasn't been going so well as I've more than gained a two pounder myself.

"You shouldn't have brought these," I say.

"You don't have to eat them all — it's called have one or two, besides which this gesture is in direct opposition to the management's attempts to control us," my co-worker says. She is becoming more politically militant than me, sparking my envy. At this point, relations between us have soured considerably due to how much information we have on each other in regards to theft (several grand apiece), and the fact that we both have failed to research any socialist parties or other groups that could serve either as an outlet for our frustration or change of our position. It's worse than when nearly the same thing happened when I worked at the museum and my co-workers and I just about wanted each other dead while chanting our lines.

On the balcony, gale-force winds and palm frond smacks upon the face, I stand brooding, picking up on people's awkward dinner energies and wishing they were just someone else entirely. I sketch a dinner scene onto a cardboard canvas in hopes of turning it into a painting, but draw a bowl of lemons so large it takes up the entire board, and the hand I've attempted to rest on one lemon looks more like Vienna sausage fingers. I tie a silken scarf round the balcony doorknob and study the wind's effect on the fabric.

On our date the man I'd seduced at the supplement shop drives into populated crosswalks and yells fuck you to the crosswalk's population who are asking him what in God's name he's doing. "I'd say the same thing," I tell him as he hits a jaywalker who really does deserve it. We smile at each other. We tour the old neighborhood of his mother's mind and come upon a witch's house. The witch does psychic table readings with balls and wands and cards. She tells me about my ability to pick up on the city's psychic malaise. She tells me to quit with the marble blocks and paints and nooses and knob scarves since my inescapable sense of dissatisfaction and lack of self-respect will prevent me from producing work of quality, before launching into the stories of the old neighborhoods of her own mind. The stories are a snooze but somewhat Charmant in the way mean witches who tell you you are lost and tell you to stop doing everything you're doing can be Charmant.

Cluuuuuuuuunk — that's the sound of the new man hitting pedestrians.

Weeeoooooooohweeeeeeoooooooohhh — that's the sound of police sirens in some distance.

The man and I make an appearance at the museum currently showing the illuminated manuscripts of monk fever dreams, most of which depict phallic altars and penis fountains and male orgies and hand jobs given under robes and potatoes used as butt plugs. The phallic illuminations in the galleries are a dream of the man's come true. I never cared for illuminated manuscripts, but over time people have cared for them and kept around and displayed them, so clearly it appeals to many, like the man.

"It shows someone with skill taking the time!" The man says, purchasing a book of the illuminated manuscripts from the gift shop.

"The illustrated depiction of sex fantasies is relevant only to the particular fantasy-haver, and maybe whoever is enamored of the fantasy-haver," I tell him. He is not into discourse regarding persistent matters of the day as much as the last man, but he believes in preservation-through-conversation of people's interpretations and personal visions over time. After the illuminated manuscripts, we visit the tar pits because he likes the idea of children's field trips and things getting stuck in the tar. He throws some newspapers into the tar pit and we are chased a little by a security guard, then let off with a warning. They have no cafeteria and I am displeased. With low blood sugar I tell him the only thing I really like, and actually love, are the old-style cafeterias of California with aging waitresses in short brown dresses and brown pantyhose and bright white bows on their asses and their bright white shoes over their hose and their sun damaged skin that makes their wrinkles tenfold and their eyeliner stuck between the creases illuminated, such as manuscripts. These old cafeterias (not the tar pits) are the great things of the city — you can order orange juice in paper boxes. Something sad for the cafeteria waitresses was that they were writers but became mothers and then all kinds of stuff from kids books seeped into their work — which was never truly work because it was altogether unread. It was the age of misogyny in the form of anti-working-mother-with-literary-dreams. "Some call it sad but I just call it most likely," I say. "They refill your coffee and tell you about their lost work and don't know where it went asunder, using words like that."

"Okay," he says. "No need to belabor the subject." We don't go to one of the good cafeterias since they're far away and usually found by chance.

At the big house I'm asked about my new date that I have brought along.

"I don't know," I say. "He is a gentleman in that he bought my coffee. He also bought an expensive book of penis drawings, so he has some money." The man makes the rounds showing people the book. Some really like it.

Drinks are offered and our clothes come off. My date doesn't look at me until after everyone is finished, his gaze pausing to study the other men and women's bodies, his erection bobbing up and down. Tired, everyone watches TV together. During the evening float rebroadcast we witness the groundhog; seeing his own shadow, the city rejoices because it is never winter. They made a float of him in terra-cotta-colored roses, resembling either a bowel movement or a highly knobby cane; I can see it clearly on the woman's truly high-def TV. "I'd like the purpose to reveal itself to me," I announce to everyone as they pop bottles in various stages of dress and undress and begin preparations for round two. "In any form," I say. "The woman's house is empty of reason or cause, and I cannot get a grasp of the overall physical arrangement when things are in full swing, and I don't know how to use any of this information or what to do with the imagery," I say. Someone puts a video of our last group action on the high-def TV. "This should provide a clearer picture," she says.

"That's not what I had in mind," I say, unable to watch myself.

I'm asked to leave the house before round two by the man I brought, even though we'd done so many cultural things together, even though I had become somewhat known and desired for my frequent menstruation within the particular circle.

"I'd to like to experience the group alone," the man tells me.

"That's reasonable," I say.

I receive a personal message from the woman of the house: It just isn't working out, is it?

Upon the balcony I'm caught by energies of the city's people trying to remember what they were doing in the first place. I look over my remaining materials that have not been taken by the wind and spread throughout the city. Even some of my heavier materials have vanished. I consider abandoning the ABP koan as it's caused more problems than solutions, though a tip in the handbook states that things become much, much, much harder, and then impossibly hard, before (possibly) getting better (for very few), especially where koan effects are concerned. I began undertaking with paints and other things so as to have something with dimensions and products outside of myself that would be self-defining in nature or else by proxy. Someone had mentioned post-deskilling, and perhaps my current method is what, as this person suggested, will follow, and as such I needn't worry because I'm ahead of the times. My Gene Autry bust remains unfinished; having only seen one or two statues of his image in places I passed by car, I didn't remember his face well, or what he'd done, and his likeness never really came through the chipped form of raw marble. I place the marble block on the balcony ledge for the wind, when it's ready. In the face of memory, I remember the subject matter that I was going to call my work and had done immersive research in: paintings of multiples in sex situations. Only to realize it had been done before and so many times in total. As well as I've never been good with the human figure.

SARAH SARCHIN, *UNTITLED*, 2014, CHARCOAL AND GRAPHITE ON PAPER, 30 X 22 INCHES.

HOARDERS: STEVEN

KATE DURBIN

STEVEN
Anaheim, California

My name is Steven and I'm 48 years old Van Gogh's "Starry Night" poster

I'll definitely take one of these broken snow globe of the Eiffel Tower

I've always had the problem of clutter Styrofoam cup

I've thought about why I do this uh my parents divorced and my father was kind of uh distant toward me poster of the Beatles crossing the street

I'm not quite sure if he really liked me when I was a child pumpkin liquefying on the kitchen floor

My father had given me a train set but he had to sell it because they needed the money Styrofoam cup

And so I remember having good times with my father and that mouse droppings on pillow

And so that disappeared broken oscillating fan

When I first moved into this apartment it wasn't organized Styrofoam cup

So I just would like put things in a temporary spot Styrofoam cup

And since everything was in a temporary mode Scrabble board with no letter tiles

That's the way I felt about everything else, including the garbage mountain of plastic shopping bags

When I have been in a place where there was a pathway to where I was sleeping, I felt uneasy lamp with no shade and no bulb

And this way I'm kind of secure because if someone were to try to get to me they would have to go through a lot of stuff, make a lot of noise dead Christmas tree

It's not healthy, I understand that Styrofoam cup

There should be no fear involved open box of Ritz crackers

You just you just have to let go exploding Dreyer's ice cream box with chocolate oozing out

This is really tough frozen tamales with green mold

It's all human excrement and stuff like that can of gasoline

And it's tough plate of rotting chicken and flies

This is so embarrassing for human beings and for dirty, stuffed Donald Duck

I want to keep that comb, I've been looking for that ceiling-high stack of newspapers

A few toiletries and stuff but the rest is unwashed clothes spilling down the stairs

Does not support mind body and soul empty birdcage with bird shit

A new man deflated Happy Birthday balloon

Thinking I'm never gonna let it get this way again Styrofoam cup

How I got into this mess in the first place is almost beyond duct tape

You know I can't understand Domino's pizza boxes

I let it get this bad broken Brita filter

It's really amazing Quizno's cup

This house is not a home McDonald's McFlurry cup

I've had this problem my whole entire life See No Evil, Hear No Evil, Speak No Evil piggy bank

I'm going to have a new life shit running down sides of the toilet

I'm going to have the life I've always wanted and never had "Bridesmaids" DVD box with no DVD

BRITTANY NEIMETH, *THE HOUSES, #1*, 2016, DIGITAL ARCHIVAL PRINT FROM MEDIUM FORMAT PHOTOGRAPH, 40 X 50 INCHES. WWW.BRITTANYNEIMETH.COM

HOARDERS: LINDA

KATE DURBIN

LINDA
Los Angeles, California

My name is Linda and I'm 51 years old Class of 2006 polar bear

You know there's just something about um getting a good deal "Finding Nemo" statue

The health and beauty aisle here is a really good bargain nine hundred pink Bic razors

When you get a good deal there's a little charge that you get with that
Swarovski crystal encrusted Care Bear

What I'm seeing is there is an addiction connection to that Big Lots shopping bag

I might have to get some of these wire hangers

Growing up it was always cluttery Victoria's Secret shopping bags

My parents were children of the Depression era and pretty much there's a lot of things that you save because ya might need 'em TY Beanie Babies

This is good stuff Smirnoff Ice box

This a good price two thousand teddy bears

And look at this, it's a Hello Kitty keychain still inside the package

I have that whole depression thinking because I think I better get this now because I may not able to get it tomorrow fifty alarm clocks

You know we might run out of rhinestone cat collars

I tried to find my identity in everybody else and in things and more Sudoku puzzle books

Until you know I got to this point where now I'm being smothered by melted Yankee candles

Save that because it's a Schwinn and I can sell this box of shoes without pairs

At one time, there was a husband here antique life vest

This one I'll keep because it smells good thirty-year-old Dove Soap bar

Obviously living like this you don't want anybody to see that you
live like this ocean of Hallmark wrapping paper

It's like this deep dark secret copy of "What to Expect When You're Expecting"

Who wants to show anyone baby clothes with the tags still on

This is humiliating overturned dining chairs

It's wretched cat litter everywhere

Yeah come look at my pit, you know chewed animal bones

If this isn't hell, I don't know what is Hoover fusion vacuum cleaner

Hoarding is so ugly, you know who wants to HOARD dead wasps

Even just the word is like echhhhhhhhhhhhhhhhhhhhhhhhhhhhhhhhhh

BRITTANY NEIMETH, *THE HOUSES, #3*, 2016, DIGITAL ARCHIVAL PRINT FROM MEDIUM FORMAT PHOTOGRAPH, 40 X 50 INCHES. WWW.BRITTANYNEIMETH.COM

AMITA BHATT, *A FANTASTIC COLLISION OF THE THREE WORLDS-XVIII*, 2013, CHARCOAL AND OIL STICK ON CANVAS, 9 X 12 FEET ©AMITA BHATT

EXCERPT FROM

THE NERVOUS SYSTEM

KIM CALDER

MY ARM WAS covered in bruises the size of thumbprints. The side of my face hurt from being pushed up against the pole you tied me to like I'd been clocked good once, the tenderness extending down my neck and into my shoulder. You tied my hands and bent me over, asked if I could slide my hands further down, and so I slid them almost to the floor and felt my face against the hard surface.

When the side of my face began to ache, I worried I'd be bruised there and wouldn't be able to hide it. The bruise never appeared, but if it had, what I worried was that other people would see the bruise and recognize it for what it was but not for what it wasn't. One does not go to work, the world, with a bruised face, a fat lip, the mark of another's hands on them, without provoking a series of unanswerable questions.

This is the first time I have been tied to a pole. More significantly, this is only the second time I have been tied up. Somehow my mind doesn't go to the way my friend, Shevawn, was tied to a chair, gagged, and then strangled to death in an abandoned building. It is beyond me why I have chosen to trust a man in this way, is there a thing beyond me, operating? How foolish; how liberating; how potentially deadly.

As I understand it, a lover is a person one can speak frankly to. You can beg a lover to tie you up or a lover can propose to tie you up. I learned as a baby that needs are a thing best kept quiet and deep, so I often fail at speaking frankly, and when I do, I am afraid. Often, I don't know what it is I want or want to say.

When you read this I want you to know I am trying my best to speak straight, not sideways. I'm trying not to speak different out both sides of my mouth while swallowing the center. In other words, I promise not to tell you I love you and then kill you.

The US Department of Justice collected data on violent crimes in 2011. Approximately 90.5 percent of known/convicted murders were committed by men. This did not surprise me; here is what did: Only 23.2 percent of murder victims were women. Then I looked at the statistics for victims of other violent crimes, like rape, and my surprise disappeared.

If a great enough shock to the system kills the relationship a woman has with her body, this is not death exactly but it is the death of a way of being. Often the body becomes a carrier not only of the mind but also of a constant untouchable pain. The explanations of the mechanisms by which these pains appear are abstract, but the hurt and the how come are dishearteningly clear.

How unlikely, then, that two women in my life have been murdered.

Here are their names.

Shevawn Geoghegan. Bound, gagged, and strangled to death by her so-called ex-boyfriend and his two friends as part of a "Satanic ritual" in 1998.

Judy Calder (my mother). Stabbed to death by her so-called friend in 2007 over an outstanding loan.

If you want to know more, which everyone always does, you can search for their names online and you will find them, and, eventually, me. You'll see a 16-year old girl, and then a 24-year-old girl, trying to talk about murder, as I am now still trying to do, and stumbling again.

During the trial of my mother's murderer the defense played videos of detectives interrogating him. He moved rapidly from topic to topic (he was a good talker, he even stayed with us for days after my mom went missing pretending to help look for her).

When I said I never wanted to talk to you out both sides of my mouth while swallowing the center this is the kind of talking I mean. He said don't worry we will find her I have people canvassing the city, she is like a mother to me. The other side of his mouth said after I stabbed her I dumped her body in the desert and I will run as soon as the chance presents itself.

In the defense's tapes he talked and talked out both sides and then settled on me. He explained how my mother believed, fundamentally, that I was "unstable." I had sat through any number of his lies, so it was a shock to hear something that might be true. But he was using "unstable" to mean untrustworthy. I am always unstable but I also trust myself.

Two murders. Two bodies. Two courtrooms. I have struggled with talking about these when I write "poetry." It turns out that when there are multiples of these things it becomes very difficult for a reader to differentiate them in a manuscript. I tried numbering them, or referring to "my first courtroom" or "the first time a woman I love was cut from the world." This, however, does not work so well because when there are multiples of these things it becomes impossible, or at least not useful, to differentiate them. I think of the two deaths as "bookends" holding together a decade that is largely a blur — the morning after they found Shevawn's body, I woke up and started drinking. I didn't stop until just nine months before my mother was killed, at the end of that decade.

When the world has been mostly a blur for half your life, it becomes hard to differentiate anything from anything.

In a process called limbic regulation, a mother's emotional brain trains her baby's nervous system to be like hers. For me, this meant that from the start, my wiring was loosely connected, already shorting out, "fragile." Ready to blow unless I were to live an impossibly lucky life, which neither of us did.

It's funny how the family and friends of people who were murdered are referred to as "survivors of a violent crime."

I wasn't there when either Shevawn or my mother were killed. I have only seen it happen by listening to witnesses who were accomplices to varying degrees — a man watching the knife go in my mother's chest through a cracked door from the other room; the man who tied the restraints and helped prepare Shevawn for sacrifice.

I am not a survivor of these particular violent crimes. What I survive in this case are the stories told by other people and all the details of circumstance and intension outlined by the prosecution and witnesses in the courtrooms. I wonder what blows my body took as I sat on those wooden pews with the eyes of the jury on me, seeing me seeing them die. Each revelation a well-landed punch.

The one, and I hope last, time a man hit me in the face it was a good shot, and I just looked back at him, as if it had been inevitable. I called in sick to work. I laughed when a counselor gave me the number for a women's shelter. I remember the look on his face the next morning when he saw my face better than I remember being hit. A look of self-hatred and sadness, of wishing to be swallowed up immediately by the earth. It matched my own so well. Some men who commit violence are what we might think of as monsters, displaying a total lack of empathy and remorse, and others are just human, fucked-up. Human and fucked-up.

Just because this was the first time this man hit me doesn't mean it was the first time he'd been violent, it just means it was the time he used his fist. When I was young I wrote a book of poems mostly about this man and failed to mention the fist. The book ended with another man who died last year when his heart stopped suddenly. That other man once didn't listen when I said no. I stopped him suddenly and named his actions out loud, I said, this is about to be rape. He couldn't believe he could be the thing he was in that moment, but he was. He was a good man who saved my life many times. He loved me when I needed to be loved even if I didn't know I needed it or how to ask. Isn't rape always about power? It should not be such a dangerous thing not to know your own desires, but he had kept hearing me say no when I meant yes. This situation was not equivalent to any other, but he didn't see that.

I thought, after finishing that book, that I was done writing about men, and about fucking, but their violence keeps intruding into my life, into my writing, so I'm calling it in, opening the door and putting on a pot of fucking coffee. I'm asking, what do I do? What if I could jack the whole fucked state of my body into pleasure? What if I could take this incessant state of fighting and flying and make it about fucking, which is maybe to say, make it about love, or desire, or whatever you call it when you know what you want and it's given without assumption or claim.

The man I am fucking says, I love women, and this phrase outlines a fundamental difference between us, as I will never be able to say, I love men.

But by deploying him as a category here, maybe I objectify and instrumentalize him in the same way he did me.

Maybe giving a man permission to tie me up and fuck me lets me experience all these events, as I naïvely imagine, safely. A place of refuge containing the violence of life where you can stop the tragedy before it occurs, make it an experiment about pleasure, a game where you can press pause if you need to.

After my mom was stabbed to death and left in the desert, my body responded in an understandable and predictably symbolic way. I'd curl up for a week at a time racked with sharp cramps so painful it was hard to walk. Now I wonder: Was the process of limbic regulation continuing, was my body feeling her death along with her?

Then the pain spread everywhere, and expanded its symbolic range. A constant, infuriating dull ache; shooting pains in my legs when I walked; migraines lasting for days where I could only lie in a dark room. I started falling asleep driving even after 14 hours of sleep. I couldn't not sleep, all I wanted to do was sleep. It was as if my body had given up, had enough. I found myself in a very shitty vessel with a very enormous sea to cross.

It is especially confusing to love a body that seems to hate you, that seems to have established a system of resisting its connection to the mind in a way that can't be overridden. Living in a traumatized body can feel like dragging a corpse around all the time; grief can feel like dragging a corpse around all the time; surely this is not a mistake.

Writing this is a way of asking my body, what do you want, and also asking the bodies I'm dragging around, what do you want?

This is why I love reading and writing theory because it asks the world what it wants, what it wants to be. It is first and foremost a lover's discourse.

I spend a lot of time asking my body, as you would a lover you wanted to please, what do you want? And like me, when in the past, a lover has asked me what I want, my body seems not to know, to have a hard time articulating anything but hurt. I immerse myself in hot water and wait. I try to take my medicine in a responsible way, and I wait. I ask again, the answer is always the same.

I kept trying so hard to get my body out of pain and then suddenly a man pulled my hair hard, wrapped his hands around my throat when we were fucking, tied me up, and my body was in heaven. Simple math — a negative times a negative makes a positive, right?

I did not try to stop him when it happened, I didn't want it to stop, the last thing I wanted was for it to stop. What a joy, to have this violence happening to me and instead of wondering why won't it stop, please not one more body decomposed beyond recognition in the desert or with a neck covered in bruises the shape of hands and slathered in makeup (there was not enough to cover them, there just isn't), feeling instead I never want it to stop.

Just as the baby's nervous system absorbs how to be from the mother, starting in the womb, the baby also learns about being through the attitude in which its needs are met by the mother. If the mother fulfills a need (like breastfeeding) merely out of obligation, the baby will sense her reluctance and experience the interaction as toxic rather than nurturing.

Therefore those who are undermothered (I hardly had one even when I technically had one) are constantly ashamed of their needs, feeling them primarily as a burden others do not want to meet, and so when I had them met, in one way, without having even to say what they were, this felt like a kind of intuitive grace on the part of the other. A gift.

It occurred to me less, perhaps, than it should have, that the similarities could be a real fucking problem, and that there may be no safe spaces for women in this world. ❖

AMITA BHATT, *A FANTASTIC COLLISION OF THE THREE WORLDS-XXVI*, 2016,
CHARCOAL AND OIL STICK ON CANVAS, 9 X 12 FEET ©AMITA BHATT

PRODIGAL SAYS LISTEN

LYNN MELNICK

I didn't notice the tunnels
dug around me
that would save me
having to hitch
recklessly away

but it's too late now
I guess because
I guess before
I was too busy trying
to hold on to my body

to worry
about destroying it but
in any case
I love the fortuity
I love the plenty of rope

back here on the wide
bright boulevards
and anyway it's exciting
how I grew
to have a good life.

I bring my middle age
to your window
and watch downtown watch
a gal on a roof
in a pool.

That's my body
whether I fuck it or be it so
cheers! to my return.
You said
don't wear that

kind of mouth
at your age, don't.
I said, listen, I was a child
until I was a whore
but now I'm just a tourist

in this headliner town
and my body
has remained
incredible
though I punished it.

TINSELTOWN

LYNN MELNICK

All the beige apartment buildings
with absurd little windows
despite the sun they could let in:
I get those buildings.
I formed all my bad ideas in those buildings
then I took them to the streets.
Yesterday
I stood and I snapped
the outdated GIRLS DANCE sign overhanging
a parking lot outside a pop-up restaurant
people feel so fancy about
they are willing to wait to eat
when they never want for food.

Girls did dance, I assure you. Late century
we all felt the pop-metal backbeat
supersede our heart, but
simpler times!
I mean, as kids we could walk into bars
throw some quarters into vending
and pull the knob out for Kents
or whatever mistakenly fell.
The bartenders didn't not give us matches.
We didn't not give them blow jobs.
This was before the sharing economy
or else what if
maybe we invented it.

KIM TRUONG, *DEPART I*, 2010, PORCELAIN, LIMESTONE, DIMENSIONS BETWEEN 5 AND 21 INCHES. PHOTO: MICHAEL UNDERWOOD

RITUAL

JILL KATO

THE BACKCOUNTRY ROADS are crude. The road we drive is narrow. There are three and a half million acres of open desert, but I still have to keep my eyes on the road to make sure this gigantic RV stays on path.

"Where are we going?" I ask, but the only response I receive is the wheeze of Walter's breath. I look over to the passenger's seat and see he's sleeping. His mouth cracks open, his head tilts back, his jaw slack.

I know where we're going, so I don't know why I asked. We're driving to Death Valley's southwest corner, a remote area, 275 miles from our home. We set our itinerary months ago. Perhaps my question was a reflex for conversation. Perhaps it was to hear my own voice, something besides the engine's hum and Walter's lungs.

I should have realized Walter was asleep. Although the wheeze of his laboring lungs remains constant, the sound of his breathing has changed, each breath a bit deeper, more drawn out, but still full of interruptions.

Walter sleeps. I drive. This has been our routine for the past two days.

For the last half hour, the view through the RV's windshield hasn't changed. The Panamint Mountains line the horizon. A bit closer, layers of sandstone and mudstone cover the clay. The hills are the colors of latte and cocoa, and speckled before them, gray-green creosote bushes texture the dirt. Besides the flight of the occasional turkey buzzard, the only movement I see comes from the dust that rips from our tires and into the air behind us like a dissolving tail.

We've rented the RV. It's called the Keystone Motor Coach Outlaw. We like the name. It's 39 feet long and has an interior height of 84 inches. The bathroom has residential-style fixtures and a skylight over the shower with polished porcelain tile floors. It's outfitted with a king-sized bed with memory foam and a 48-inch LED HDTV. At home, we sleep on a 17-year-old queen mattress and watch a TV the size of a microwave. We're living our last days in luxury.

The Keystone Outlaw may look like a fancy hotel room on wheels, but it's a nightmare to drive. I brace my lower back with my palm, straighten my posture, straighten the seat. I attempt to adjust everything in order to lessen this ache.

I'm looking for an abandoned mine called Widerman. It's deep in the backcountry, about 34 miles from the 180. Walter and I like to imagine ourselves among the pioneers, the adventurers, those that mined for silver and gold. We like to imagine ourselves among the type of people who rode in on horses and weren't scared off by places called Funeral Mountains, Deadman Pass, or Coffin Peak. We wanted a place far from tourists, a place in the valley all our own. There are a thousand miles of backcountry road and in the summer, these roads can go weeks without a single vehicle passing by.

When we were younger, but not young, we would joke about how we would die. I said I would die from complications from a fall. I'd trip on the upturned corner of our oriental rug, break a wrist, maybe a hip, be sent to a hospital where I'd catch pneumonia and die. That's how two out of my four grandparents went. That's how my father died as well. "Why mess with tradition?" I'd say. Back then, it was easy to be flippant.

We agreed it was most likely that Walter would die from trauma. He'd engage in some sort of reckless activity, some sort of adventure where he'd get himself in way over his head. He would die trying to hike the Nā Pali Coast or die trying to sail from Miami to Turks and Caicos after only a half-day course on a keelboat. That sounded like how Walter would go.

Nowadays, the sound of Walter's whistling lungs accompanies everything we do. We watch reruns of *Law & Order*, eat hot dogs with sweet relish, and walk laps around the park — through all of this, Walter's lungs whistle. They provide the disjointed rhythm of our days.

I drive. The lungs whistle. I imagine his lungs filling slowly with watery sputum, a glass carafe sloshing back and forth as I drive. Today, are his lungs a quarter full? A third? Halfway there? It doesn't matter. Either way, Walter will drown.

Lung cancer. Not a fall from a Hawaiian cliff or a capsized boat, but mucinous bronchioloalveolar carcinoma. That's what will get him in the end.

Walter's breath sputters. It's enough to wake him, and his eyelids flit. I rest my hand on his arm, over his paper skin, and he falls back to sleep. He slouches in the bulky passenger seat, his hips slip to the edge, his twig arms droop over the armrest, his head flops over in my direction. His hair used to have the shine and rich color of oiled leather, but now it grows out of his head like dried grass, what's left of it anyway. His arms are bald, so are his legs, and underarms too. A small sprout still grows from his groin, but otherwise, his body is like one of those hairless Sphynx cats. My body is like this too.

Our skin no longer fits the frame of our bodies. It hangs and gathers off our bones like the oversized sweaters we wear to keep warm. We're covered with liver spots, skin tags, bruises, and Band-Aids. Our skin looks and acts like tissue paper, and when we bump into things — corners of tables, edges of counters, chairs not completely pushed in — it tears. We're old, older than old people were when we were young. Old people were 50 back then.

Walter is on a high dose of steroids, which makes his skin even thinner. I grabbed him once, when he lost his balance, and after I pulled my hand away, five finger-sized bruises appeared. "You've been working out," he said. I tried to laugh.

We're beginning a slow ascent into the Nelson Range. The Keystone Motor Coach Outlaw struggles to climb. The road has narrowed and branches of digger pine and bristlecones brush the side of the RV. The Panamints are to the southwest, as is Telescope Peak. The road splits and an abandoned yellow water truck sits just off to the side at the fork. The yellow water truck means we're headed in the right direction. I turn right and reduce our speed from 45 to 15.

Walter got the idea from the Inuit. It's popular belief that when an Inuit gets too old and infirm they are set adrift on a piece of iceberg and float out to sea. The theory is that the conditions they lived in were so harsh and required so much manpower to survive, the community couldn't afford to support those who could no longer contribute to the whole.

The image of the ice raft is romantic, but not true. Only in extreme circumstances, when the tribe was confronted with famine, say, the aged and infirm may have ended their lives, but in those rare circumstances, they probably just wandered out into the snow.

When Walter told me this was how he wanted to go, I thought he was putting me on or trying to get my goat in some perverse sort of way. Then I thought this was just another one of his dreams that he rashly embraced and then abandoned, like when he quit his teaching job at the community college so we could live in East Asia or when 10 years ago, he traded in his Toyota Avalon for a Harley-Davidson Road King and expected me to hop on the back. We ended up traveling for three weeks, all the vacation time my job would allow, and Walter went back to teaching like he never quit. The Road King sits in our garage, under a plastic cover, with less than a thousand miles on the odometer.

So when Walter announced his plans for his Inuit death, I thought he'd talk about it for a few days and move on to another one of his grand plans. When he didn't, when I realized he wasn't going to let this go, I was incensed. I grabbed my keys and drove over to Lucille's Café on Glassell Street and sat there for half a day. I drank mugs of decaf coffee and ate a piece of pecan pie and then a piece of lemon meringue, and then ordered a third piece to take home because I felt guilty for taking up a table without ordering more.

Instead of giving me time to cool down, the time I spent at Lucille's worked me up even more. By the time I arrived home and found Walter sitting at the kitchen table with a glass of scotch and a blank Sudoku puzzle in front of him, I was ready to let him have it. I was ready to tell him what I thought about his asinine plan. But instead of actually speaking, I took the boxed pie and flung it hard across the table. My aim was off and instead of crashing into Walter's newspaper and scotch, it veered right, flew off the table, and onto the floor. Walter looked at me and then turned to look at the box. He pushed himself away from the table with scotch in hand and pulled out a couple of forks from the utensil drawer. Next, he ripped off a couple of paper towels from the roll by the sink and held onto the handle of the cabinet as he lowered himself to the ground.

"Oh good, I was hoping it was pie," he said as he opened the box, his back against the cabinets, his feet splayed wide in front of him. Walter folded the paper towels in half, laid one on the ground next to him, and placed a fork on top. "Or at least I think it's pie," he said as he drew his fork across the cream coated sides of the box. "Mmm, banana cream," he said after he took a bite.

He waved me over, and even though I was still angry I got down on the floor next to him. He offered me a bite, but I shook my head, partly out of anger, partly because the idea of more pie made my stomach turn.

"What about our gambling trip to the state line? We go every year. And we're planning on going to that avocado festival. Where was that? Carpinteria? Or what about your Tuesday breakfasts with the guys?" But after I said the last thing, I wanted to take it back. Because of course, the guys had just become *a* guy, Walter's friend Tony. Richard passed away last year and Roy, eight months before that.

"I can't go to hospice again," Walter said. He shifted his weight like he was trying to get up. I put a hand on his arm.

"What do you need? I'll get it," I said.

"Johnnie Walker," he said.

I got the scotch from the table and then lowered one knee, then the other, back to the floor. He held out his glass and I refilled it with a generous pour.

"I don't want to be in pain and I want to know when," he said as he took a sip of the whiskey. "I don't want to die in a hospice bed."

Hospice, hospice, hospice. It was touch and go for a while. Before Walter brought up the Inuits, we had talked about hospice, round and round, for weeks. Walter had had to have a feeding tube inserted down his nose for nourishment. "And do you want to know the worst of it," he had said. "It felt like drowning." We're not religious people, but I know Walter likes the idea of having his death connected to something grander, something that would make his life seem bigger and more dignified than a hospice bed.

On the road, we approach a sign made from wooden slats with its carved letters painted black. It reads:

Widerman Pass
Caution:
No Tow Service.

We drive on, but at an even slower pace. I keep the Outlaw rolling under 10 miles per hour. There's about a foot of space between the RV's tires and the edge of the hill. According to the dashboard, the temperature outside is 117 degrees.

Two months ago, I had a nosebleed that wouldn't stop. We went to the doctor's office and that's when they found it — melanoma, in my left sinus. Metastatic to the lungs and liver and maybe my brain, but they can't tell yet. When I found out, I couldn't believe it. "Melanoma is from the sun," I said to the doctor, pleading.

"You can get melanoma anywhere," he said. "You can get it in your colon or your vagina." I thought it was weird that he picked those two examples, but I got the point.

The melanoma is terminal, but for now, I feel tired, but fine. I've had to be more active around the house since Walter got sick, so I feel in better shape than I have in years. For now, I feel strong enough to drive this giant RV for a few days through these backcountry roads, cook our meals, and set up camp. The doctor recommended chemotherapy — treatments with semi-pronounceable names like ipilimumab and nivolumab — but I don't want to go down that road. They say the best I can hope for with this treatment is an extension of a few extra months beyond the year I'd perhaps have. But without Walter, what's the point.

Every aspect of our days are lived in tandem. We're like marionettes pulled by the same strings. Our lives are insular. It's just us. Since the desert is closer than the arctic and since Walter's lungs are filling with water, the dryness of the desert has more appeal. It's best if we walk out as one. Tomorrow, we'll do the Inuit walk together.

We did our research. Aided with pills, terminal dehydration is a peaceful way to go. The dehydration process itself produces an analgesic or numbing effect. It causes a reduction in swelling and it makes people with tumors, people like Walter, more comfortable. We found a study that said hospice nurses rate death by terminal dehydration as a high-quality death. They gave it an eight out of nine, with nine being a "very good death." Walter and I agreed that eight out of nine is probably as good as it's going to get.

I see some dark rotted wood set into a hillside and then the metal frame of a wagon and a few barrels, both rusted. This must be it. The location is remote and there's a cluster of Mesquite trees that don't offer much shade, but are better than nothing. I steer the Outlaw off the road, under the trees and away from the rusted debris. The giant vehicle lumbers side to side over the rocky loam and my body rocks side to side in my seat. Walter's body lumbers left and right in unison with mine, but still he sleeps.

I try to avoid the patches of creosote bushes, but it's hard, and I end up rolling over some of the smaller plants. I hear stones pop under the tires as I slow the RV to a stop. The Outlaw is new, but the door still makes a sucking creak that screeches through the quiet of the desert.

This is the second day we've been in the valley, but every time I step out of the air-conditioned RV, I'm shocked by the heat. It's hot, but it could be hotter considering it's July. I reach my arms over head to stretch my back, and roll my neck in circles. It feels good to stand.

I raise my hand to my forehead like a visor and look around. Next to the rusted barrels is a pair of rusted troughs, and nestled in the hills are ore car tracks and shafts, more evidence of the Widerman mine. Warm brown hills hug us on three sides and on the fourth, there's a view of Saline Valley. The hills ripple out from where I stand in brown waves. The white strata of clouds that lay atop the hills are crisp and bright. The sky's blue is deeper, more saturated than the brackish air back home in Orange. I'm glad the view is nice for Walter's sake. He always appreciates a good view.

I roll out the awning attached to the Outlaw's roof and open the back door to unpack what we'll need to set up camp. I grab our two folding lawn chairs made of aluminum frames and woven nylon straps and hook one on each arm. I carry them out and set them up under the shade. I fetch the portable fire pit made of polished copper that we bought from the hardware store last week and place it between the chairs. We've also brought a couple of Duraflame logs guaranteed to last for more than four hours. In this heat, the thought of a fire seems ridiculous, but Walter likes the idea of a fire, so a fire we will have.

The passenger's door creaks open and Walter steps out. The sun is beginning to fall, its color carroty and viscous.

"Annie?" Walter calls. "We're here?"

"We're here," I say. I've worked up quite a sweat setting up camp and I wipe my forehead with the back of my sleeve.

"Here, here?" Walter's water-filled chest affects his voice too. It's quieter and full of gravel.

"Here, here," I say, like I'm announcing the arrival of our destination to a child.

I go to Walter, still standing next to the open door, revving up from his nap, trying to get his bearings. I smooth his hair with my fingers and thread my arm through his.

"Was the drive okay? How're you holding up?" he asks.

"Just fine, love," I say.

"Annie, look at that view," he says and walks closer to the hill's edge. "What are those, the Panamints?"

"I think so," I say, following him, shadowing his walk.

Walter turns around, takes in our surroundings. "Hey, there're the mine shafts." He starts walking toward them and I know if I don't distract him he'll wander in and explore.

"Let's enjoy the view," I say, and Walter doesn't object. I take his arm and lead him over to the chairs I've set up outside. We sit down like old people: scoot the back of our knees to the edge of the chairs, hold onto the armrests, and lower our bottoms down slowly. Walter lays a forearm over the armrest and I lay my arm over his. We kick out our feet in the dirt and listen to the disjointed rhythm of his breathing.

Forty-nine years, that's how long we've been married. I remember thinking Walter was so worldly back then. He taught anthropology at the community college where I worked as a file clerk. He read *The Economist* and wore skinny black ties and Italian boots. He didn't just talk about baseball or complain about his boss, like the other men I knew, but he actually wanted to talk about things going on in this world, like the race riots and

GALA PORRAS-KIM, *FUTURE SPACES REPLICATE EARLIER SPACES (STACKED ACROBATS 2)*, 2016, GRAPHITE ON PAPER, MAHOGANY. COURTESY OF THE ARTIST AND COMMONWEALTH & COUNCIL

Vietnam, and cared about what I thought about them, too.

The first time we had sex was after a department meeting, against the olive-colored filing cabinets behind my desk. After that, this now-dying man with paper skin and no hair would take me into his office and we'd have sex on his desk, in his chair, a balancing act involving a stool. I'd meet him at his office and we'd shut the door. We'd make plans to meet in the office supply closet down on the basement floor and knock shoulder blades and hips into reams of letterhead and boxes of Swingline paper fasteners. Other times, during my lunch break, we'd drive our cars out to where Hillgate dead-ends and hop in the back seat and have good sloppy sex. But that was decades ago, when we couldn't keep our hands off each other and Walter was proposing all sorts of crazy stunts.

Nowadays, besides our daily walk, most of what we do is sit. We're sitting now, out here in this backcountry, where what hits you after the heat is the quiet. It's miles and miles of open land and then there is silence. The silence must get to Walter too because he starts singing, "So what, da-dah-da-dah-da-dah-dum-dum, so what,"as he squeezes the beat out in my hand. He braces his weight on the armrest and pushes himself up.

This is what Walter does every night. He sings "So What" even before he turns on the player, picks up the needle, and places it on the disc.

Here in the desert, we still play Miles from the same vinyl we've been listening to for years and on the same turntable we listen to at home. We play it on the turntable we loaded into the Outlaw a few days ago so we can continue our own little ritual, out here in the desert.

Walter walks to the Outlaw's door; his steps are shorter than they used to be. He climbs up the steps into the RV, and after a couple of minutes, the trumpet and bass intro drifts through the screen door. I hear him rattling around in the galley and I know he's fixing himself a drink. I know he's pouring Johnnie Walker Black in a short squat glass and then swirling the amber liquid in a circle.

"Why don't you pour one of those for me," I yell out to him from the lawn chair. I pull my collar in and out from my chest, trying to fan myself with my shirt.

He doesn't say anything, but I know he's surprised. I imagine him smiling. I imagine his eyebrows raised.

He comes back outside with two tumblers. I take one and wave the liquor under my nose and pull it away. I jerk back my head and crinkle my face. I've never gotten used to the smell of hard alcohol. To me, it smells like medicine.

"I'll finish it if you can't," he says.

Walter drinks and I start dinner. I go inside and pull out the New York strip from the mini fridge under the counter. Walter's sense of taste is going and the light flavor of a filet mignon would taste like nothing to him, so we went with the strip steak.

When we were planning our last meal, we considered other, more exotic and indulgent dishes — a spicy lamb curry with jasmine rice, a buffet of chocolate éclairs, petit fours, and macarons, or escargot and caviar, because we always thought of those last two things as the epitome of fancy. We enjoyed discussing the possibilities of our last meal, but in the end we agreed we wanted everything to be the same, just a regular night, so we settled on steak.

"So What" ends and "Freddie Freeloader" starts. Walter goes over to the record player and pulls the needle back to the first track. "So what," he sings along with Miles's trumpet. He wraps one hand around my waist and holds his other to my wrist, even though I'm holding a plate of bloody steaks. He tries to spin me around. I laugh and playfully swat him on the back with my free hand.

"Walter, you're making me spill," I say.

"So what," Walter sings in response.

I set the dish on the counter so we can take a few spins around the narrow cabin of the RV. Walter swings me back to the galley and continues to dance with his glass of scotch, but his dance is interrupted by coughs. He taps his fingers against his chest, trying to loosen that damn phlegm.

"You okay?" I ask.

"Nothing that a little walk in the desert can't fix." He lowers his glass from his lips. "I'm sorry," he says, "Not funny."

"Not funny at all," I say.

We're not cavalier about our decision. We've thought about it for months. Back at our house in Orange, we've left instructions for our lawyer and handwritten letters to our few friends who remain. We've left a letter for our closest relative, Walter's niece, a divorcée who lives with her two kids in Cincinnati. I've turned the water valve clockwise with a wrench and put the mail on hold. Keys have been labeled, computer passwords written in block letters on index cards. I've laid out our papers, keys, and passwords on Walter's oak desk. Everything one needs to close out our lives is collated in neat vertical rows.

I know what will greet us tomorrow won't be pleasant. This land is harsh and shouldn't be toyed with. I know gritty flash floods can wear down walls of stone like liquid sandpaper and that tourists wander out into the desert, get lost, and die with some frequency. We respect the threat this land holds. I noticed that after we made our decision on our Inuit death, we stopped calling the desert by its name. We refer to it as the "desert" or the "valley." The "death" part is too on the nose.

Walter is using the toilet, which happens quite a lot now. I take out the hibachi and light a pile of coals. When the coals are hot, I lay the steaks and some asparagus on the grill. I take out the folding table and set it up in front of the fire pit and cover it with the same everyday tablecloth we use at home, not the one we save for guests. We want everything to be the same.

"Why don't you open the cab," I call out to Walter, but he's beaten me to it. He steps out of the RV with two glasses of the Stag's Leap Cask 23 Cabernet Sauvignon and the bottle wedged under his armpit. "What would you buy if this was your last night on earth?" we asked the guy at the wine shop. Besides the luxury of the Keystone Outlaw, this bottle of wine is our other splurge. Neither of us knows wine, but we spent $240 on the bottle because the guy at the shop said it was good.

"How is it?" I ask. Walter raises a glass toward my lips and tips the wine into my mouth. It makes my mouth pucker and my tongue feels covered with cloves. The cabernet has a strong, more aggressive sort of taste than what I'm used to, but to me, it still just tastes like wine. I say "delicious," and lick my lips for effect.

"We're really living it up, aren't we Annie," Walter says.

Walter goes back into the RV and returns with a couple of forks and steak knives poking out of his left pant pocket and cloth napkins draped out of his right. Like always, he sets the table while I cook.

"A few more minutes," I call out. The sky stains pink before it stains purple, but that color in between looks lovely like a hibiscus.

I go inside and take out a Tupperware from the fridge and scoop a couple of mounds of my homemade potato salad on real plates, not paper. I added a lot of eggs and extra pickles, just like Walter likes. I place Walter's pills on the rim of his plate like they're part of his meal. The gel caps and chalky horse pills roll into each other to form a colorful little line — morphine, Lasix, Metoprolol, the list goes on. He's also wearing a Fentanyl patch on his upper arm to help with the pain. There's just Lisinopril for me. Even though it's our last night, we've decided it's best to take our pills. We want to be able to carry out our walk.

Walter tops-off our wine glasses and we sit down to eat. In this light, his face blends into the dusk. "Cheers," he says, raising his glass. We drink wine, not water. It's all part of the dehydration process, all part of things we've discussed before, like why we're sitting outside and not in the Outlaw with its generator-powered A/C.

"Cheers," I say and we clink glasses and lean in to kiss, like we always do.

Walter takes a big bite of the potato salad. "I'm sure going to miss this," he says.

I take a bite of the strip steak. It's a tad overdone, but still good. "Thank God," I say. "I was terrified I'd ruin them." Walter cuts a piece of the steak and pulls it off the fork with his teeth.

"Perfect," he says, his mouth full.

Walter is a romantic and that's why he's blind. He's an anthropologist and very well knows the Inuit didn't float away on icebergs, but when he imagines our Inuit death, he sees us drifting on an ice float in the Arctic Sea. He doesn't see the unpleasant truth. He ignores the fact that when we go, our bodies will let go of everything they're holding inside. He doesn't see us dying on burning sand, shit and piss leaking from our bodies. He doesn't see our skin shriveling from our bones and our bones dissolving into dirt, nothing more than carrion for the turkey buzzards I saw on the drive in. He only imagines us holding hands, the ice raft floating over water and the view from our backs, looking up at a big Arctic sky.

The sun clings to its last lambent glow. Walter eats all of his potato salad, but only half of the asparagus and steak. My plate is clean and I'm half-tempted to help Walter finish his, but I want to save room for dessert. I carry our dinner plates away and return with two pieces of marionberry pie I had hidden away in a cooler. It's another one of Walter's favorites.

"Surprise," I say as I put Walter's piece in front of him.

"Where the devil did you hide this," he says. His first bite is big, but he doesn't come close to finishing the whole piece.

After dessert, I put away the hibachi and fold up the table. I dump the hot coals in a tin box I've stored in back. The land is full of grayness and of dust, so I feel like I have to wipe everything down with a towel before I pack it in the RV. Walter takes Miles off the player and puts him away in his sleeve. Chet goes on next. Walter starts in on the dishes and I dry and stack them in the cabinet, like we always do.

After we clean up, we go back outside and sit in the folding chairs looking across the valley to the hills we can no longer see. I light the Duraflame log and we intertwine our arms like braided dough. I set my wine glass down in the sand. It's been a long time since we tried to finish a bottle of wine and it takes us longer than it used to.

"Are you scared?" I ask.

Walter takes off his glasses and rubs the bridge of his nose. "No," he says. "I'm ready." But he averts his gaze and I wonder how ready he actually is. "How about you?"

"I'm ready," I say, although I get up to fetch the bottle of wine from the inside of the RV though neither of our glasses are empty.

"Annie, come. Sit back down. Stay here with me." He reaches out his hand and then gets up and takes the bottle from me. "There's no need for that now," he says and strokes his hand across my back.

"Fine, okay," I say.

I sit back down, return my arm to Walter's, but I can't stop my mind from jumping a day ahead and wondering where we'll be and what we'll feel or hopefully not feel. Out here in this heat, will our bodies not cool after we're gone? Will they actually become hotter? Hotter than the sand?

We talk about Harold Grossman's colonoscopy and then Susan Ikari's adoption of a Whippet dog, but our conversation never really catches. We, who never lack for conversation, have trouble conversing. After a long silence, Walter says, "Bed?"

It's late, or rather, late for us. We push our bodies up from the flimsy chairs, fold them, and take them inside. I shovel sand over the Duralog and the fire sizzles and then smokes after the last flames fizzle out. Inside, I pack up the clothes we will no longer need and stack them neat in our luggage. Walter goes around the RV and collects the old issues of *Sunset* magazine we never got around to reading, and slides them in the pocket of our luggage. I throw away the wine bottle we finally finished and wash the wine glasses and put them in the cupboard. We set out what we'll need for tomorrow — khaki pants with pockets for our pain pills, just enough water to swallow those pills, thick cotton socks, long-sleeved collared shirts, wrap-around sunglasses, and wide-brimmed hats — all laid out neatly on the sofa ready to go.

I change into my cotton pajamas and Walter uses the sink in the bathroom to brush his teeth. He's taking longer than usual, so I go in and check what he's doing. He's shaving, running a razor blade over the coarse sparse hairs that remain. He's already nicked himself under his jaw and a spot of blood, a deep carmine red forms and blossoms.

After Walter is finished in the bathroom, I squeeze in. I wash my face, floss, brush, and gargle, like I always do, everything the same. When I finish, I go to the bedroom. Walter is lying on the bed, under a sheet, and staring at the ceiling. I turn the lights off and slip under the sheet next to him and look up at the ceiling too.

In the dark, I feel the mattress shift and the humidity of Walter's breath on my cheek. I turn and our mouths meet. His lips feel tight and cracked over mine and as we kiss I moisten his peeling lips with the saliva from my mouth. I reach my hand to his face and the hair around his temples feels damp, like he ran a wet comb through it moments ago in that tiny bathroom. On the mattress, our bodies come together, wrap around each other, our skin over our bones, our skin pressed together. We're together and we kiss, but not for long because Walter coughs again. His breath sounds brittle and failing, his lungs rattle with coins. I rub my palm over his chest and sink into the nook of his shoulder.

"Maybe tomorrow isn't a good idea," I want to say, "maybe the day after tomorrow." But what's the point of bringing these things up again. We've agreed that we want tonight to be a regular night and I've agreed that we'll go on this Inuit walk together.

In the bed of the Keystone Outlaw, Walter says how much he loves me and I say how much I love him and I begin apologizing, about how, now that I think about it, the New York strip steak was a little tough and then say I'm sorry for bringing his blue pajamas and not his green striped ones that are actually his favorite, as if I'm working up to apologize for any possible failings from our whole lives together, but Walter stops me from speaking with his dry chapped lips. We roll on our backs, and we grasp each other's arms until the rhythm of Walter's breathing changes and I know he's asleep.

I listen to Walter's jagged breath. If I fall asleep, I don't remember, but sometime during the night, the mattress sinks and then rises. Walter walks out of the bedroom and closes the door behind him. He closes the door so softly, I barely hear it latch. I hear the floor of the Outlaw creak as he walks to the bathroom and then a long pause before I hear his stream of urine. The Outlaw may be big for an RV, but it's still a tight space, and I can hear his every movement around the cabin. I hear soft shuffling somewhere beyond the door. I hear a soft grumble when I imagine he's taken a seat. But it's not until I hear the ripping sound of him lifting the straps of his Velcro shoes that I know for sure what he's doing.

Out in the main cabin, I hear another quiet groan. The body that has become lighter with age becomes increasingly harder for him to lift. I imagine he's pushed himself up from the sofa and then I hear his short steps approaching the bedroom door. I hear the door open and I feel his eyes on me before I feel his touch. He lays the tips of his fingers on my shoulder and then I hear his wheezy breath lower to my face and feel his mouth press lightly against my temple like a seal. I want to roll over, I want to open my eyes, but I do nothing. The seal of his lips lifts from my temple. I hear his wheezing retreat. I hear his shoes back toward the door. Still, I do nothing. It's not until I hear the Outlaw's main door close behind him that I shift in bed. I hear him leave and still, I do nothing.

I wonder if Walter planned to sneak out all along. I wonder if he knew I would have cold feet and wanted to spare me the torture of having to decide. The agreed-upon-but-never-discussed lie was that we were going on the Inuit walk together. We knew that I would never allow him to do this unless I thought I was walking too. Perhaps we both needed that illusion to get through our last night. Perhaps that's why this last trip has always been about Walter. Steaks for Walter. A bonfire for Walter. Walter's favorite potato salad. Walter's favorite pie. Or maybe I'm trying to let myself off the hook.

I imagine him out there alone, humming, "So what, da-dah, da-dah…" and I imagine me here, tomorrow, alone. And still I do nothing.

WINTER: APHORISMS

SARAH VAP

Drones are probably killing someone right now.

High intensity sonar training exercises are causing blood to pour from the ears of whales right now.

Wi-fi clouds are surrounding me right now as badly as I could I.

Who is innocent. And for how long.

Do I love going beyond what I know.

Do I love looking closely at something I don't understand until it has changed me.

Do I love looking closely at something invisible until it has changed me.

Lorca said but hurry, let's entwine ourselves as one, our mouth broken, our soul bitten by love, so time discovers us safely destroyed

Fanny Howe said my brain is a baby.

The molecular holiness of, and invisibility of, and divisibility of.

The understoodness of.

Drones are probably killing someone right now.

It sounds like they are killing someone right now.

They're killing someone for protection.

Safely destroyed and speaking to each other about the bright and otherworldly.

Garbage all around the world now flipping or spinning.
Writing brings no relief.

We are drinking glasses of water with blood in it and looking at each other as if to say what should we do?

I dreamed that the pipes below our home were bleeding, oozing blood into our water.

Our pipes were our own rotting veins.

As if our water supply. Our distressed conditions.

I dreamed I kept phoning up a childhood love and saying nothing until he screamed
my name into the phone again and again.

In that dream I was in a movie theater and everyone could hear him screaming my name except me.

I came to this place to find you. Sometimes I feel as if I have.

Networks within networks, cogs within wheels and inside there, more wheels or liquids,
and there – liquid among the babies. Is that you.

Liquid among the babies a part is sweetest.

Among the cogs or at the cogs themselves a part is sweetest.

What part is sweetest I don't know what I'm saying I am obscure to myself but he is brightly shining.

Oh, him. Him and all of his little.

When the first baby arrived listen to me.

When the first baby arrived listen to me he was so little that I began to have enemies.

Reversed, flipped back the violence rounded and ample fell on my knees to pray.
To rip off the balls with my teeth.

He is so little I.

Now that this little baby is so little I want to kill my enemies.

Now that these babies are so little I have found a rage equal to the love I have I.

I have begun to love to the utmost I have begun utmostly to hate.

Despise detest abhor want to kill to the utmost I.

He is so little the thrill of hope.

Fall on your knees. Oh hear the. So tiny so sweet my god –

When the first baby arrived I began to feel hope as more porous, more tenuous, more endangered, larger, moody, repetitive, dull, ferocious.

Now something mattered more than something about to be born. When the first baby arrived I saw that the assemblage grew.

I saw the expansion of assemblages and the budding of assemblages the cracking open
of new assemblages whose trajectories, like the slipping open of the eggs like the dome's
like the drone's like the sonar's I.

As badly as I could I.

And so among these assemblages and comprising these assemblages how do I extricate myself from these assemblages how do I extricate the tiny baby from the cogs that have made him from I.

When the first baby arrived I saw the passion of the assemblages.

When the first baby arrived I began to devise the killing of my enemies: executives at
chemical companies oil companies pipeline lobbyists all mining companies all billionaires
packs of dogs Monsanto anyone who makes the precariousness not stop.

When the first baby arrived I began to beg I sharpened my teeth I fell on my knees.

I thought about what you did not do for one of these least ones you did not do for me
and began to, I didn't sleep.

I began to ask what is the most one, what is the least one, and what is this sweetness
at the core of my rage I.

I didn't wake either, I did on my knees. Nighttime.

Or early morning. Or late afternoon all the time I did a little dream of, I, just like the ones I.

When the first baby arrived I imagined bending over reaching back to spread my butt cheeks
as far apart as I could to show you something I.

Practically begging my soul to reveal itself I.

Open open at the center part I.

When the second baby arrived I began to pray as well as to beg as well as to want to kill even more enemies: education policy makers shrimp boat captains World Bank executives Monsanto military sonar experts executives at health insurance companies anyone who makes the precariousness not stop.

I began the long supplication but also I am even more ready to kill. Dismember or mutilate I.

I began to not asleep began to not awake and ready to kill the drone operators drone designers drone engineers drone profiteers drone lovers drone fans everyone and anyone surrounding
sonar deployment in oceans I.

The invisible killer murk around us I want to kill I.

There are guns everywhere I. He is so tiny I.

For the time being I am the center of everything that screams and teems when the babies
arrived I began to oh holy slime. Into my brains into the center of the mucous of love, my god.

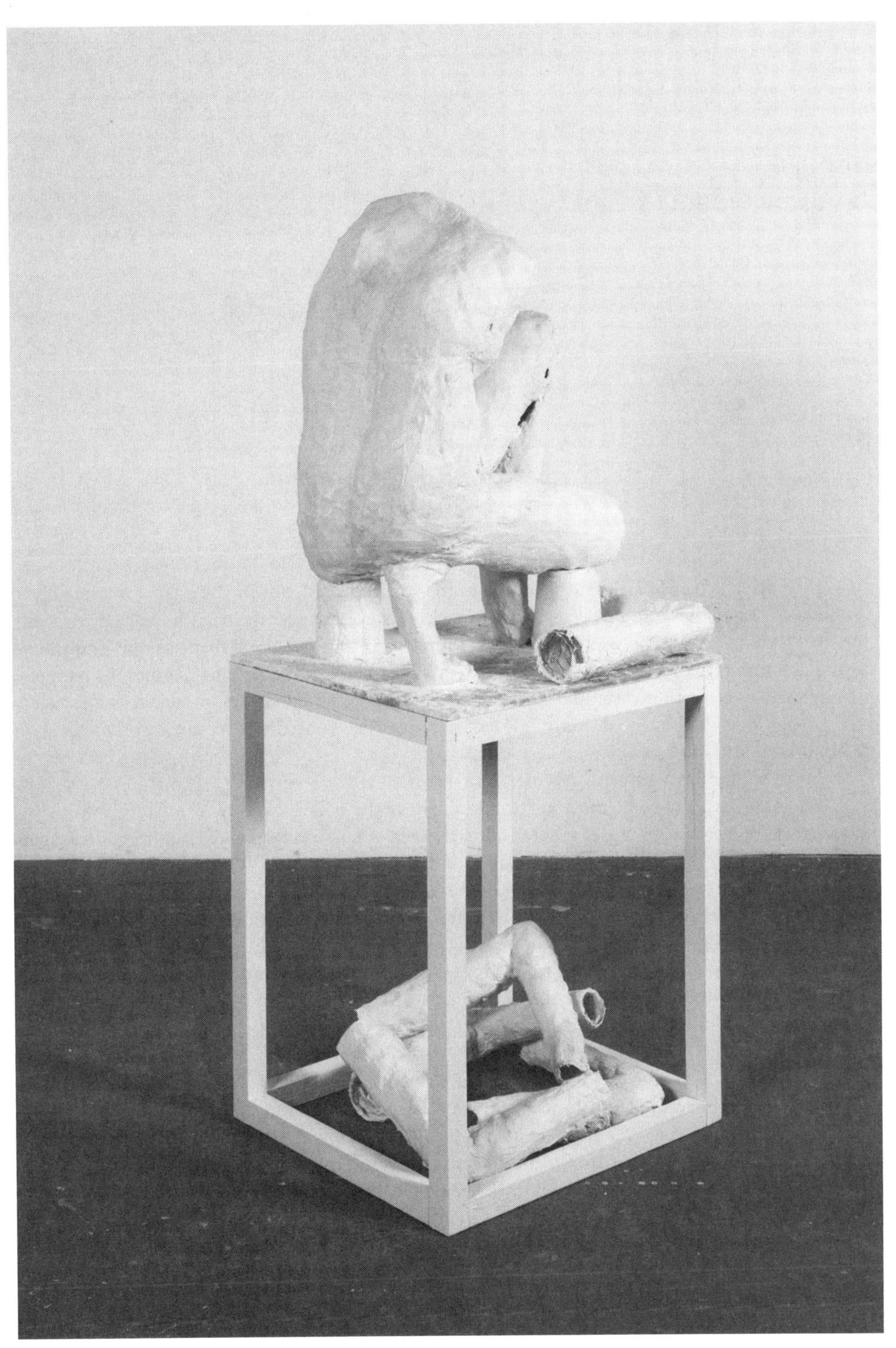

SARAH SARCHIN, *A LASS AND A LACK II*, 2016,
WIRE, PLASTER, BURLAP, WOOD, ACRYLIC, 58 X 20 X 24 INCHES.

INSIDE

ANDREW NICHOLLS

I'VE REPLACED PEOPLE and been the one replaced, but in the past they were always gone when I got there or vice versa. At Immaculatus, we have a one-month overlap with our predecessors not knowing what the deal is, then boom they get their surprise one month bye-bye. For some reason the place doesn't want the Cuthberts guessing what's going to happen to them. They want them stunned like a pair of tranquilized zoo bears, punched in the face, staggering forward, paws out, asking, *Why?* After they're booted out we cuckoo into their one-bedroom faculty bungalow.

None of this sits well with Nicole.

We taxi to a leafy, semi-outdoor restaurant near the college, where Van Morrison is singing a song like he's trying to chisel all around the edges of something he can't quite get the shape of right. Nicole gives me the big eyes and a nudge: *isn't that them?* A couple sits at a swayback table over the patio drainage hole. They look like their Facebook photos. Him: Tall and bald, *185 friends*, mostly of starchy professorial mien. Her: Linda Ronstadt, 1975, lipstick-topped, Bond girl. Half her *28 friends* had the same surname and were holding babies and/or barbecue equipment. As we slide past them to our table, they start talking more pointedly, *you* this and that, familiar switchbacks on Coupledom Road leading to the Vista Point of a meaty argument. The wife says, "I'm a simple country girl, you knew that." She's got the local accent, her voice small and precise.

"Or is your thing like this table," he drawls. "Is it like a scale, so the wrong balance ruins your fragile equilibrium, if you follow me, sweetheart?" Pretending to be polite at the salty end, the feint of a quick, cruel man. I'm your wife, she says, screwing the paper sleeve from her straw into a worm, then flicking a drop of water on it to watch it writhe. He bulls his head behind the menu, either food indecision or saying, *Where's a precipice I can fling you off?* A waitress kneels to wedge a matchbook under the table. Nicole, with her back to them, gives me wide eyes. I stroke her arm to say, long flight, long drive, let's just soak up what's left of the day.

Immaculatus insists faculty be married and that spouses *participate in campus affairs*. "It's what we prefer," administrator Jeanette told me on the phone. She hinted with a *we're-all-Christians-here* Southern intimacy that something about the Cuthbert wife, her appearance or language, had unsettled the Carolinian devout.

They found me teaching at UC Riverside in Southern California, a hot 45-minute commute from our Fullerton apartment. Plus tutoring at home, which Nicole hates. At Immaculatus we'll live on site, rent all-in. I heard that and right away felt I could breathe. Plus only one thesis student in the first semester, bla-*dow*. "The main thing is that everyone has an opportunity to *serve*," Jeanette said, italicizing the word with a telephone smile like a housebound woman stroking a trapped cat. I was so happy about the gig I didn't think about the discomfort of teaching for four weeks with the guy I'm bouncing.

Nicole, second-generation Los Angelena, is baptized and has no criminal record, apparently the core bona fides for an Immaculatus faculty wife. She co-runs a poetry blog that hasn't run anything sodomistic in months and she helps out at some small presses. Except for teaching prisoners to write free verse about people they've bludgeoned, she can keep doing what she does on the east coast as easily as from California, plus visit the birthplaces of Dickinson, Whitman, and others I've only heard of through her reading to me in bed about meadows and grosbeaks. She's not comfortable with me agreeing to these terms with the school, the not-telling, the sly dancing-around, the "treachery." She says it's not too late to formulate demands of my own referencing straightforwardness, decency. Maybe I can ask for a meadow I tell her.

Monday night we meet everyone at a get-together in the Cocoa-Puff-yellow staff room: crackers and cheese and soft jazz on a boom box held together with flaking brown tape. Jeanette, who looks like the banker's secretary on *The Beverly Hillbillies*, introduces me to my soon-to-be-predecessor. We get a better look at Mikkel Cuthbert, pronounced Michael, who is tall and round-headed with a tan that goes all the way up his nose and an unfortunate skull cleft off to starboard that looks like when he was born they were out of forceps and had to use a melon baller. He wears a blond silk jacket that he tells my admiring wife came from Hong Kong. He's smiling but I can picture him looming down creaking stairs with a shovel to brain whomever dared enter his sticky subterranean domain. Perhaps this is projection on my part. Terri Cuthbert in her nice-smelling white top makes me think of a bird. Not her posture or face so much as a beady-eyed blankness. A willingness to please, implying something pent. When she speaks about how sweet she finds it at the college her opinions feel ladled from a well of nothing. Her page-boy is a red that hair doesn't come in. Nicole's is long and honey-brown and swings like Barbie's naughty playmate Midge's. In my dreams she has three freckles on each side of her nose — six, the hard way. I drew them on her once, with a red felt-tip, in a Fullerton motel when our apartment building was being gassed for termites and we had sex on a balcony above a pool full of frolicking Midwesterners.

Mikkel and I talk east coast blahblah and 20th-century European philosophy. "Hume, Kant, Locke," he says. "They aren't crazy about the existentialists, the Vienna Circle, they'll steer you around that." He tells us we ought to come by their place Friday and see how they've got themselves fixed. Nicole brims. "Sure," I say, "sounds great." With obvious budget cuts like the cafeteria A/C turned off, I don't know how he doesn't see it coming. Offhand I'd guess they're saving six, seven grand a year by replacing him with me. Them with us.

I teach his students for five days, dicking around with a coyly auxiliary Phil 101 curriculum. Immaculatus has 600-and-something friendly if creepily deferential students. *As we learned last term, sir,* that kind of thing. LEGO haircuts and iPhones glued to their arms. Would it be cruel to say they have little to think about, and little to think it with? No, they're all right. One night I dream Cuthbert's chasing me through the maze from

The Shining with a glue gun. Nicole says a couple more weeks and they'll be gone, then you'll be king of the roost, Mister Rooster.

Friday night we try our luck at some Scratcher tickets, argue lightly about this and that, pick the lint off each other, and walk over. I don't want to do this but here it is. There are fake Colonial lights on fluted verdigris poles about the campus, with red Rape Alert buttons. Nicole swings my hand and asks, "What do you suppose is wrong with her?" "Maybe," I say, "we'll find out when she comes out of the bedroom in a big wooden rabbit mask." Anything with creepy rituals unplugs something in Nicole. When she's fretful she becomes 16, and I want to chase her across a playground. "Don't," she says, girl-punching my arm, "or I'll tell them about you-know-what, you bet your dick I will."

Their section of faculty housing is west of campus, eight duplex huts shaded by wisteria and bragging catalpa, with a gravel walkway between. Low-volt lights on fake pagodas, moisture-retaining cedar chips. Nicer than I pictured. From outside their screen door I hear Mikkel say, "As if that's part of my job." *The Cuthberts*, it says on a piece of heraldic plastic.

He takes our wine orders, she does the tour. When the women are both in the bathroom my cell rings. It's Kiley, Jeanette's little assistant. According to our next-unit neighbor in the place they've put us, our smoke detector's bleeping. Kiley talks in halty questions as if upsetting me might get her fired by Jesus. If we're not there, she says, she has orders to call the fire department. Don't, I say, it's always the battery. The battery, I tell her, Kiley, go pull the battery. I say we'll be out till at least 10 and I give her permission to enter. I picture her in the dark with her boyfriend, both of them testing our bed with nervous knees.

I squeeze in the bathroom with Terri and Nicole. Each foot of their big enamel tub sits in a Tupperware thing of skanky liquid. "Palmetto beetles," Terri sniffs, "I thought I left them in Florida." Nicole ruffles a lip and peers in one of the cups. Terri's shorter than Nicole but feels more present, more here-in-the-room. Pretending to look around, I study her glossy head, the white canoes of her calves. Mikkel makes kitchen noises. Shelves line their hallway, oak built-ins. I'm a sucker for a dark hall full of books. In the main room, someone's hung a wide African batik thing in a frame: a lamb and a lion getting along. It looks like a *Watchtower* cover: the crayon-rainbow view of heaven. And the tenured shall lie down with the adjunct.

Nicole and I go around the glass coffee table and perch on the couch, bus-style. Terri takes the chair facing us, sitting straight down like placing a pawn. There's something kabuki about her. I feel glum and guarded so I grin like an idiot. Any time two faculty couples get together to drink I'm reminded of the Albee play. Terri and Nicole start right off chatting while Mikkel butlers a tray of something. He's 10 years older than the three of us, call it 44. I picture his long frame diagonalizing the door a month from now, cradling one elbow with a Joan Didion scowl, watching me carry in our bedding, saying, "Well I guess you know where *that* goes, professor."

Holding my wine I spill a few chocolate peanut things and they roll toward Terri's knees. She gets a frowny look and twists towards the hubby. Mikkel says, "Wayne, no, leave it, let me get it." He sets down his martini, corrals the candy and drops it in the bowl. "Terri has a thing," he says. "An, uh, inability we have to kinda work around." Here it is, I think: rabbit mask. Nicole shows me her I love you *but* face. Terri scoops her shrimp across a battlefield of red sauce. "In fact," Mikkel says, "I'd be interested to know what you two think about it." He puts a hand on his wife's shoulder and Terri looks up at him like, here we go. I picture the four of us out on the path in 20 minutes, grassy-kneed, brawling like on *Project Runway*.

"She has an agnosia," he says, gentling it into the air like a just-opened Cabernet. The *she* under discussion blows on her bloody shrimp, her small face neutral under the red bangs, knees together. "Or if you like a phobia. She calls it her *difficulty*. She's unable to put things inside other things."

I stare him in one eye and swallow. Their fridge cycles on.

"Basically, Terri can't make her hands put an object inside another object. Tube, box, hole." He gives her a look, like staring at your used car that was a great deal when you bought it but summer comes and you find out it's got no A/C. "She can take things *out* or put them *beside*, but she can't put a thing in another thing." I look boldly at her face and she upshifts to an elevator smile. *Well, here we all are.* When he swings back and forth to see what we think — Wayne? Nicole? Wayne? — his skull cleft catches the light from a gastric orange globe chained to the ceiling.

Nicole does the thing where you pretend your mouth's full. "Oh," I say. I don't know what I imagined when Jeanette said the wife makes folks around campus uncomfortable. Tourette's maybe? I had a dean who fired his head of HR for obsessing over 9/11. Who knows what a person will decide one day itches his stump.

"Some uncharitably imagine it as willfulness," Terri says, looking at Nicole. "But we don't consider stutterers willful!" She pats her husband's hand where he's clamped it on her scapula.

"I didn't notice it on our first date." Mikkel works his big tongue around his mouth. "Even on the second date there was just a, say, an *awkwardness* when it came time to put Terri's leftovers in the Styrofoam takeaway thing."

"Clamshell," she says.

"She pointed and said, *Would you mind?* I scooped it in for her." I hear Jeanette's voice in my ear, each Carolina syllable stretched over a drying rack. *Some folks fit in, others don't. Ah'm sure you have this where you teach.* Nicole does a jaw-grip smiley like she has hold of a Frisbee with her lips.

"She can get her arms into sleeves or her foot in a sock so long as she doesn't look. Obviously she can put food in her mouth. Just not a letter in a postbox, a fork in a drawer, groceries in a bag." There's a gentlemen-of-the-jury quality to this. "At least she can't stick a knife in me."

"Dear, I could always pull a wire around your neck."

"Ha! That's true!" He touches her wine. "Since we told them, would you *prefer* — ?" She nods like, *Of course I would, Dimbo.* I don't get the significance of this at first. Female voices walk by the window. Nothing can make me feel I'm inside so powerfully as young women outside. I only now notice the curtains are drawn, blocking the view of catalpa pods, hobbity path. I rub the back of Nicole's hand with my thumb and fill her in on Kylie's smoke alarm call as Mikkel lumps to the kitchen and returns with an aluminum shaker and a martini glass. "Terri can't load the dishwasher, or re-box shoes in the mall. She can't put a credit card back in her wallet." Absent, but there by implication: *You see how crazy that is? Do you see why I have no hair to cover my unsightly skull dent?* He puts the martini makings on the table, pivots a heavy red club chair on one leg, and swings it to Nicole's side of the couch, facing us. My wife says, "I had an aunt who couldn't turn left. She had to do car trips as all right turns. She also pulled her hair out in clumps. She had to wear a do-rag thing." I had never heard about this.

He inverts the tumbler over a glass with a toothpick and olives. "Years ago I wrote to Oliver Sacks at Columbia. He said it was new to him. There's no name for it even."

"Mikkel sometimes thinks I'm faking."

"*Well.*" His eyebrows up to a God in the rafters.

"But I ask you, why would I? I mean, what would it get me?"

"My dear, you might think it makes you more mysteriously alluring." Swinging his glass like a Bond villain.

Nicole asks, "If you don't mind me asking, when did it start?" Terri swivels her neck, trying to get her head into the diving helmet of a recollection. I eye the batik lion and its trusting lamby pal.

"So far as I can remember I've always been this way." She takes toothpick-plus-olives from her glass, licks the vodka off with a pointy tongue, and hands Mikkel the plastic sword. He holds it at waist level like a leash. She sips, then holds out her drink. He drops the olives back in her glass and falls into the club chair. "Her parents weren't very observant is all I can say. They thought she was either messy or forgetful."

Nicole asks, "How long have you two been together?" If she met the Queen of England she'd ask this.

"Six years," he says. "We met on a cruise ship. Singles Dance Night, drinks *o'erlooking the ocean*. We were married at my parents' house in Florida, then I got this offer and up we came. We're both from around here originally."

"Wayne and I met five years ago," Nicole tells them. It's more like four and a half. The fact of it is, we're not actually technically married, but Immaculatus doesn't check. As she starts on that story, changing The Viper Room to "a small concert hall in L.A.," I excuse myself and pad to the hallway, passing the bedroom's open door. There we are on the King-sized, me on the right, Nicole on the left and this evening just a squirmy memory. We'll need a second reading lamp. His speech just now seems to me like a recap not of his wife's handicap but of the nobility of his own suffering. On the other hand, they're firing them for this? I picture a staff meeting, the squeamish trying to justify their hostility with reference to Christian attributes found lacking. *If that Samaritan thing happens again, she can't put the guy in an ambulance.* What about tampons, I wonder crudely. What about ATM cards? Is croquet *in* or *through*?

The bathroom mirror reminds me I have a reddish beard. Nicole says it makes me look like the banjo player in a jug band. What is it, I wonder, about the people we work with? Arbitrary and picky, isolated and over-friendly, distorted like lumps of cheap glass. Two people, I decide, toeing one of the bathtub feet, need the space of more like three. That's why we hook up with other couples, looking for new territory to colonize. Perhaps, I think, this explains poetry and long sea voyages.

That must be her toothbrush lying on the sink. I flush and look quickly in their cabinet. Blade razor, cotton puffs. I don't know what I'm looking for. A prescription bottle labeled *AntiAbnormalol*?

When I come back Terri's at the kitchen getting something and he's leaning over my wife, talking low. I lower myself onto the couch. "Even the word *in* is hard for her. She'll say, Honey'd'ya put my purse *to* the trunk? If I talk about something getting inside something else, it can upset her. Bringing the *intromission* to her attention."

Terri returns with a fist of paper napkins. Someone's spilled vodka, dab dab. "Wayne, look at this." Nicole lofts a flat disc of stiff orange plastic. "Terri's trash can."

"My trash hoop." She sips defiantly.

"She puts her garbage on here and Mikkel throws it out. Isn't that clever?"

"My Galahad!"

"Your garbage stooge." He brushes his maw with the napkin wad.

Nicole rubs her own shoulders, arms crossed at the elbows. She says, "Does watching other people do it, put things inside things, make you uncomfortable?"

"A little."

"So, porn is right out," I say. I'm sorry but I can't help it.

"We've never tried watching pornography," Mikkel says. "Together."

"Oh you've got to!" Nicole laughs.

I say, "They don't have to if they don't want to." I picture him rushing out for a projector and a bedsheet. They're way too anxious to share all of this.

"Someone called you," Terri says, and points to my phone: *1 message.* I'm picking it up when my wife announces, "Wayne always wants to do it in a moving elevator, or through the chain-link fence behind a carnival." I feel cold metal on my groin in the wind. I say, "Honey? Are you feeling all right?" Nicole's laugh batters the walls. "Oh yeah, he's a major perv." She stares over my head and holds one lank of her hair like a toilet pull-chain as Mikkel refills a martini glass in front of her. When did she switch from wine to vodka?

"Have you ever forced Terri?" she asks.

"Honey ... "

"I don't mean sexually. Well, not necessarily." She snuffles a blurty laugh and covers her mouth. "I mean taken her hand and guided, like, pointed, a slice of peach on a fork back into the peach can or whatever to see if she freaks out, if her wrist wobbles, or what exactly — ?"

I cough. The Cuthberts regard each other and he turns to me. I'm pretty sure sooner or later he's going to sock me.

"Let's try it," Nicole says. "Terri, do you mind?"

"Umm," I say.

Mikkel stands. He lumbers to the kitchen. I look at Nicole. "You're kidding," I say. "Let's not do this. I mean, do we need to do this?"

Terri turns upon me a look that's half demure and half I don't know what. Pushed to the brink of something but glad to finally be there? I feel drifty. I go back to the hallway for my glass. In with their art books, I spot a volume with the spine turned to the wall. KINBAKU. Photos of erotic Japanese rope bondage. I push it back exactly where I found it. Still in the hall, I ask, "Are you comfortable with this? Terri?" By way of answering, she says, "You looked in our medicine cabinet, right?"

Where did that come from? Why ask me that? The book, the slippery red hair, the putting-inside fetish. *Oh no Mister Man, please don't.* I can't answer her. I don't know what I'm supposed to say. I cough as though I didn't hear.

Mikkel calls from the kitchen, "So you two were never caught, in an elevator or behind a carnival?" Nicole laughs at my expression poking out from the hall. We don't know these people. For God's sake, we're replacing these people.

"Not yet," Nicole boasts. "Maybe next time!" Terri laughs, a glass-chipping sound, and toasts the air. "Nicole," I say, walking back.

"Here we are!" He has something in each hand. "Not peaches but close. Tinned mandarins in syrup." Terri puts both hands over her face and does peek-a-boo. I feel like I need a minute behind something heavy, like an x-ray apron. My wife finishes her martini and nods in a loop. She's kicked her strappy shoes under the table. She does a face of being very interested in what Terri has to say, fish mouth, wide eyes. "So go on, about Jeanette? Oh, who is it she looks like? Wayne? Who did you say Jeanette looks like?"

Mikkel grinds the toothed wheel around the can. "Here we go," he says. I grasp the warming wine bottle by the neck. There's no way out, only further in like an arrow that has to be pushed past screaming bone. Terri perches her hands on her skirt-brim, going up on sitty-tippy-toe. I see her red panties. She lifts the olives from her glass and tenders them to me. Mikkel grinds at the can like he's milling wheat. These are old, he says. Were these here when we moved in? I take Terri's toothpick, my face reddening. She sips twice and holds the glass out to me, *if you please, sir*? I plop her olives back in the polar liquid and she does that French kissing-the-air thing, then lifts them out, sucks both olives off the stick with a fire-eater's flourish, laughs, pimiento blobs like doll navels in her little mouth, and drops the stick on the table.

Nicole shivers. "Don't cut yourself, Mikkel. Wayne, our apartment's on fire. I can feel it. Can't you feel it burning?"

"Our apartment's fine," I tell her.

"How do *you* know? Hey, Terri, could you — what is it Jews have? Wayne, what's it, a *goy*? Could you have one of those follow you around and put your lipstick in your purse and whatever?"

"I'm her Shabbes goy," Mikkel says, working the slick lid up and down.

"No, but, though, wouldn't a person who did that for you, wouldn't they be, and isn't Mikkel really, an extension of your arm?" Nicole tops-up her martini. "Isn't that a moral problem then, 'cause your will is creating a result the same how it would if you were making it move your hand? Has anyone asked the Jews that? Wayne, isn't that a philosophical problem? He hates when I ask him about philosophy."

"You might have something there," Mikkel says, the sharp discus between his finger and thumb.

"We've never done it on a roller-coaster," Nicole announces. "We wouldn't want Wayne flying off a corner. Into the bumper cars." Her laugh-spit hits my face.

I give her careful-eyes.

She says, "They know, Wayne."

"Know?" I pretend to be stupid but here it is.

"That we're being replaced." Terri rests her fingers on her knees. "That you're here to replace us, in all our naughty wickedness." Mikkel holds the sharp can lid like a stopwatch and licks it from bottom to top. Something in my cervical vertebrae asks for more wine but I left my glass in the hall beside the book with the Japanese girls, their labia parted with red rope. I make my face a cartoon of apology. Mikkel drops the lid on the napkin wad, leaning forward in the shiny club chair, the sides dull where his arms have sweated on them. The mandarins splay in their juice like apartment fish. "Do you know why? Did they tell you?"

What am I going to say, the college thinks his wife's a freak? Nicole digs one finger in her mouth and probes her cheek. Terri's hair lies straight like fiber-optics. The wine is hitting me, and the idea of a college wanting something suddenly strikes me as absurd. A college is buildings and lawns.

"I'm sorry," I say. "They asked me, us, not to tell you. It was a condition." I look at Nicole. "We both feel really bad about it."

Nicole kicks one of her shoes around with her toe until it points at me. "Oh! Terri! I'd love to see you golf!" she says. "Are there golf courses in South Carolina? There must be *something* here."

"How can they judge us?" Terri asks.

Mikkel says, "They're the employers, dear. They judge you, me, Nicole." But I'm the only one he looks at.

"They can't judge me," she says. "I'm just the secret second wife. Oops!" She stands, puts her hands on her hips and turns once around, holding her head, her shoulders, her elbows perfectly level. She reminds me of a pie carousel beside a cash register. Not something a person would want to do. Nicole tugs at her chest string. Mikkel leans to dump the fruit in a white cereal bowl, where the slices slither like prematurely born things. My wife picks up the silver fork and stabs it in the bowl bar-fight style. It comes up holding a dripping orange lune. She holds it out to me.

"Wayne," she says.

"Doesn't Terri hold it," I ask her. My lips click. "Isn't that your idea? Wasn't that the clever plan?"

"I want to see you do it," she says. "Prove to me you can do it, Wayne. Put the fruit cleverly in the can for all of us to learn from." She lowers her head to look up at me through her eyelashes and unties her chest string, letting the ends drop. They all three stare at me. "I didn't want to come here," Nicole says. "South Carolina wasn't my idea."

I hold the fork and look at the can. It's the easiest thing in the world to put a mandarin slice in a can. Who couldn't do that? But my arm won't move.

I feel a sky-wide sense of dislocation. The curtains, the batik, the rank smell of catalpa. I don't betray people. It isn't me who wanted this, who wrote that clause. I'm just going along, doing what people asked me to do.

I stand, my stomach heavy, and walk to the dark of their hall, our hall, and drop the fork on the bookshelf. I check my voice message. It's young Kiley. "You were right," she says. Another girl giggles in the background. The three people in the room behind me laugh. "It's some off-brand battery, Power-Lux, Power-Sux? We'll replace it tomorrow. Your apartment's fine. Temporary apartment, I mean, 'cause hey! I guess you two are family now!"

CANOEING A WORN RIVER

CALVIN BEDIENT

Alphabet of tiny paddles, is no bird sewn onto you? Is there no seating for animal leaves in your auditorium? You, laid out as for row-composition. Competition with the other transitives. You run faster in the slower water of the tentative kind.

Fleeting Charm.

The wind imprints on the water its fingertip whorls or is it "Hello"? Your paddles are amiable too, amiably altering water's complexion, in an illusion of plenitude; but, really, you yourself are the swell and ripple, for as Hegel said the outer world "is just what is not in the world." You are the "in," the paddle spank and

Finger Whorl.

Yes, one paddle forward and you're published separately, two and your motifs spread romantically. Wet and slick lick of the pen starts the flow. You cannot be the water? We are tired of hearing this. The water cannot be water, either, not even wet and slick unless you name it so. But you know, and you like it that way--arrogant and forward as you are; arranger, embellisher. You mutter something about cosmic splutter, the cruelest ecstasy. No one can prove you wrong. You wear the twisted glass shirt of the river, you take the image from Peter Redgrove, you're a thief by nature. Red grove, red grove, red grove. It's all yours now. You have no shame.

River's dissolve-speech, listen to the driveling
Discussion. It's inarticulation is the assassin.

It shifts its feet

a-tribal, a destroyer of circular ReRuns.
How is po(etry's own nonspeech consonant with water,

drifting

footprints, reeds loosed from their garrison.
Chump on the bank has model canoe for you. Form.

Mood. Other fingers. Selling colonies
In the infinite. His acrylic paintings of BankiCity

dry quickly.

Real writing enters the water. The water is not
Here for you. You are not here for the water...

The writing

is here for you In a romantic departure from the
Night is not here for you, Vessel without Venice, Shadow's End,

this headless night.

Alphabet of tiny paddles, is a bird sewed onto you,
Seating the leaves in your auditorium. A romantic

fallacy

of the cellu)lose Kind. Goes directly, goes discretely,
goes riddle, goes charm. From the standpoint

of semiotics, we propose Auspicious neutrality
aping the currents in the currents. Someone has

befriended the .

The wind steps

On the water here hello. Change in the water's sameness
is delicate delible discreek fall off a rock "The empirical river,

the outer world,

is just what is not in the world" Hegel said so. He
Discovered the laws. The World, that means, is granted

Appearance

strickly restricted.

Lean one foot Forward and you're published separately.
Like sunset on the water. Snst escapes the Rules. You're

Borne
paddling.
Your motifs
Romantically distributed.

The paddles are wet, though they cannot be water.
They are the secondary Appearance surpassing the Primary,

Now holdng its exhibition at the Durand-Ruel gallry
With greenish deliquescences by M. P. Marcel-

Béronneau

And goldfish of which there have been a lot in this year's
Exhibitions. SECONDary appearances recommend

Shine

Also. Do the Two levels of Appearance agree. Not
Strictly in yr lifetime. Do they make a Third. Do they.

Not

Lkly. "Aesthetic values are never innocent." They hum
Simultaneous. They want the world and then

Sum.

A dissolve speech, look at the driveling.
The subject is not the assassin, it shifts its feet

Post-tribal, a destroyer of circular return.
Why is this consonant with water, drifting

footprints, reeds loosed from their garrison.
Chump on the bank has model canoe for you. Form.

Mood. Other fingers. Selling the colonization
Of the infinite. His paintings dry quickly.

Writing enters the water. The water enters
You. You are not here for the water. The water

Is not here for you. The writing is here for you
In a romantic departure from the night is not here

For you, Vessel without Venice, Shadow's End.
Can it stop you stop you stop you, this headless night.

Alphabet of tiny paddles, is a bird sewed onto you,
Are the leaves seated in your auditorium.

Goes directly, goes discretely, goes riddle,
Goes charm. Auspicious neutrality in the current.

Someone has befriended the . The wind steps
On the water here hello. Changes in the water's

Sameness. "The empirical river the outer world
Is just what is not in the world" (Hegel). It is granted

Appearance. Strickly restricted. LEAN one foot
Forward and you are published separately. More freely.

Like sunset on the water. Borne. Paddling. Your motifs
Romantically distributed. The paddles are wet,

though they cannot be water. They are the secondary
Appearance surpassing in order to be Primary. They are

Its drip its recommencing shine it's undreamt of
gain. Do the two make a third. Do they.

Unknown auditorium.

A dissolve speech, look at the driveling,
Post-tribal. Pear Juice. The subject is not the assassin,

It shifts its feet, planar, a destroyer of reruns.
Why is this reed loosed from its garrison,

Consonant with water's bending knees,
drifting footprints. Tall forms on the bank.

Selling new models for you. Other hands.
Prospects for the colonization of the infinite.

Writing enters the water. The water enters
You. You are not here for the water. The water

Is not here for you. The writing is here for you
In a romantic departure from the night is not here

For you, Vessel without Venice, Shadow's End.
Can they stop you stop you stop you, this headless night's

Black buttercups on the fields of the Stygian school.
Their wings closed. Their black shadow on your chin.

Here are the birds. Here are the leaves
Here are the black birds in the black leaves.

Alphabet of tiny paddles, is a bird sewed onto you.
Going directly, going discretely, through the sky.

Are the leaves seated in your auditorium,
An auspicious neutrality. (I see them in the current,

Their green paints the underneath rocks.)

Someone has befriended the . The wind steps
On the water here hello. Quick, quick the changes

In the water's Sameness. "The empirical river.
the outer world, is just what is Not in the world"

Said Hegel. It is granted, itahasn't seized,
Appearance. Strickly restricted in originals

Beyond price. LEAN one foot
Forward and you are published separately.

More freely your canoe angles. Your motifs
Romantically distributed. Paddle, little people

Of the infinite, work in tandem with the world.
Your engaged and lifting oars are a recommencing.

A recommending. Surpasssing the Appearance

that cannot be Surpassed. Do the two then make a third.
Do they. Where. Unknown auditorium.

A dissolve-speech, listen to the driveling
Discussion. It's inarticulation is the assassin.; the assassin, it shifts its feet

Post-tribal, a destroyer of circular rERUns.
Why is this consonant with water, drifting

footprints, reeds loosed from their garrison.
Chump on the bank has model canoe for you. Form.

Mood. Other fingers. Selling the colonization
Of the infinite. His paintings dry quickly.

Writing enters the water. The water enters
You. You are not here for the water. The water

Is not here for you. The writing is here for you
In a romantic departure from the night is not here

For you, Vessel without Venice, Shadow's End.
Can it stop you stop you stop you, this headless night.

Alphabet of tiny paddles, is a bird sewed onto you,
Are the leaves seated in your auditorium.

Goes directly, goes discretely, goes riddle,
Goes charm. Auspicious neutrality in the current.

Someone has befriended the . The wind steps
On the water here hello. Changes in the water's

Sameness. "The empirical river the outer world
Is just what is not in the world" (Hegel). It is granted

Appearance. Strickly restricted. LEAN one foot
Forward and you are published separately. More freely.

Like sunset on the water. Borne. Paddling. Your motifs
Romantically distributed. The paddles are wet,

though they cannot be water. They are the secondary
Appearance surpassing in order to be Primary. They are

Its drip its recommencing shine it's undreamt of
gain. Do the two make a third. Do they.

Unknown auditorium.

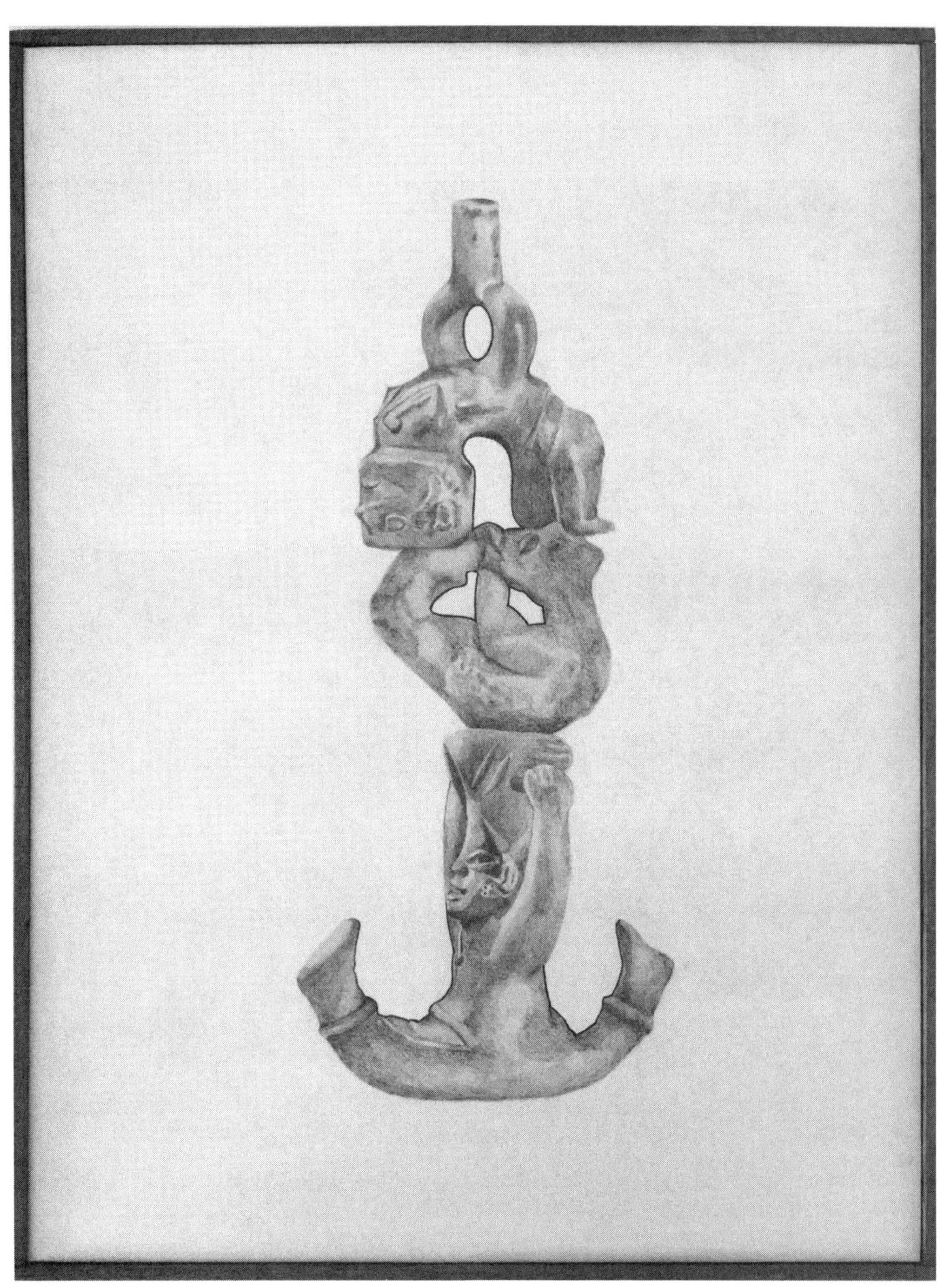

GALA PORRAS-KIM, *FUTURE SPACES REPLICATE EARLIER SPACES (STACKED ACROBATS 1)*, 2016, GRAPHITE ON PAPER, MAHOGANY. COURTESY OF THE ARTIST AND COMMONWEALTH & COUNCIL

THE AUTHOR AND HER YOUNGER BROTHER IN THEIR SHARED FRONT YARD.
PHOTO: ELVIRA VÉRTIZ, COURTESY OF THE VÉRTIZ FAMILY.

DREAM HOUSE

VICKIE VÉRTIZ

Yo soy una niña que estoy viendo un castillo muy chiquito
Esta es su casita de Vickie
Este es un carro de Vickie
Este es un cuete y una niña lo está viendo que quiere subir

— Author's journal, age six

I

IN SIXTH GRADE, my school thought I was gifted and talented, but I had never heard of college. Amá was still combing my hair into tight French braids even though other girls were wearing their hair in gravity-defying bangs. "Your clothes don't match," a girl said to me the year before. My panza made such a loud gurgling noise — how embarrassing. I had no comebacks so my cheeks glowed red and I walked away. Luckily, my sixth grade friends were also dorky and didn't have a lot of money — most of us in our town did not. Judy was a skinny cinnamon stick and Cindy's heart-shaped cheeks were teddy-bear fuzzy. They were also gifted and talented but they didn't get the certificates that proved it. I wiped off eraser bits from our table. My back was straight — I gave my full attention. I loved it when teachers would point at me and say how much they liked the way I listened. But my favorite good girl prizes were stickers, certificates, and all of the books that fit in our library.

My ambitions were about to grow.

Our teacher Ms. Strong described college, or as she might have put it, "The school you go to after high school." Ms. Strong read from a newspaper article about a local student studying architecture at a place called UCLA. Nearly 30,000 students attend UCLA, but I didn't know that then. One of us asked what an architect did and our teacher said that they built houses.

That was all she had to say. I couldn't wait to have a big house.

I never ever invited friends over to my house. We had one bedroom where two beds squeezed in across from a vanity and the closet. You had to flatten yourself sideways to go to sleep. To find our tiny house, you had to go through an alley that had garage door nalgas looking at your every few steps. Our kitchen shared a wall with the neighbors and their cockroaches. Whenever I opened a cabinet to get a glass, a few brown bugs skittered across the shelves, some took their time walking across the cabinet door. Some ended up in the clock on the wall and never made it out. Their bodies were a smudge we couldn't wipe. What if I invited a friend over and a roach would fall on her or me, a big one? Seeing those bugs every day was all I needed to know about being poor.[1]

We had enough for rent and Barbies or Hot Wheels once or twice a year. The problem was we didn't have enough money to move to a place where the landlord cared that roaches were crawling over our bags of beans. Little roach legs walking on my arm or my friend's nose? The very idea made me want to disappear. I wanted to smash the cabinets with a sledgehammer and kill those roaches for good. So when Ms. Strong said I could make my own house, I immediately saw myself in wire-rimmed glasses, drawing lines on pieces of huge white paper, an architect at this UCLA place.

"That vieja next door is a pig," Amá would say as she squished another roach with a napkin. Although the vieja neighbor has changed several times, Amá still says that today. The roaches have not moved. When I got home that night after science class, I drew my future house in a notebook; thick pencil lines showed my room bigger than my parents' and two brothers'. My room would be all pink with a canopy bed. Next to my room was a "den," something I'd only seen on TV. I wanted bright green grass in my dream home's front yard, not the cracked cement oily from Dad working on his cars that always broke down. There was no freeway near my dream house, just trees and other pretty houses.

Ms. Strong said, "If you want to go to UCLA, you have to study hard, do your homework, and get straight As." If I liked doing homework before because certificates and scratch 'n' sniff stickers made me special, from that day forward, I did long division with the serious belief that our lives depended on it.

In bed that night, I undid my braid, still worried about my hair being too Mexican and that my sneakers were from Payless, never Nike. Even though in Bell Gardens no one had a mansion, it still felt like I was supposed to have those things: big hair and name-brand clothes. But my architect dreams draped an imaginary pink canopy above my bed: a magic place called my own room where I could read and play without my baby brother bothering me. In our fantasy house, there were no roaches waiting under every chancla. My parents stretched out and slept quietly instead of making sure they didn't roll over my baby brother Chuy. They had their own room where I could not hear them snoring so loudly they sounded like the pots steaming tamales.

My panza that hurt whenever I felt bad about our little money or my too-short pants, that was the same gut that told me school would get us a dream house. That feeling was faith tied up with responsibility; by being a great student, I would take care of everyone else. With my grades and books, I would build us a bigger house.

Goodbye, roaches. And no more dead-ends.

II

Finding little to describe in the humble home, they spend a little time there; they describe it as it actually is, without really experiencing it's

1 One night, many years later, my brother Chuy woke up when a roach crawled up his arm. "When we move," he told me later, "I'm going to burn this house down."

> *primitiveness, a primitiveness which belongs to all, rich and poor alike, if they are willing to dream.*
>
> Gerard Bachelard, *The Poetics of Space*

My friend Rose wore cat-eye glasses. Rose marveled at my mother's budding botanical garden which had become our front yard: pots of aloe, ferns, and plumeria trees lined the outdoor den. Behind our house we grew corn and sugar cane, a handful of stalks, just enough for holiday ponche in December. But Rose could see things I could not.

"I wish I could build your family a second story." Rose gazed at my family's ceiling considering what it would take.

I stopped breathing.

I had brought a girl home. Rose was about 5'8". Her height transformed everything in the living room into miniatures: particleboard TV console, a sagging couch padded with blankets, our graduation photos shrank to the size of postage stamps.

"Oh girl," I said. "We don't need a second story."

I smiled. A politician's grin I didn't get to cultivate.

Just a second before, I had been proud of where we lived: a place Amá had reinvented and made her own. Behind the house they grew corn and sugar cane, a handful of stalks, just enough for holiday ponche in December.

I was supposed to get them out of here, I told myself. *I was supposed get us out of here and I couldn't do it.*

Who was going to build a second story if my brothers and I could not? There was nothing wrong with our house. But I managed to smile because I knew how to keep going, how to be pleasant even when I would rather burn down the very room I was in. Rose was white and middle class. She'd met Amá many times when she'd visited our shared apartment.

It was just a question.

"Is this it?" she asked. Something slipped inside my stomach. She had a job in affordable housing. She didn't know Amá's rent was becoming unaffordable.

"That's it!" I chirped.

"Your house is so cute!" Rose said.

I exhaled.

Rose hugged me and went back out to the garden. She worked in deconstruction. I stayed inside and fumbled for something in my purse, my dignity, for example.

I turned and Amá was still smiling when she walked into the kitchen, distracted. I shouldn't have let Rose walk into the hallway, the one that lead to the bathroom and the single, family bedroom. I had been great at disguising what I didn't have. My talent had slipped.

In seventh grade, I'd lied to my friends about having my own room. When they came over for my birthday party, one of them asked me, "Where's your room?"

I shrugged and said, "I lied. I don't have one."

"Okay!" she said. And somehow the other three girls shrugged, too. Somehow, I didn't die of shame, the hot blood rushing to my cheeks. They didn't seem to care — perhaps they were thirsty. I offered them cherry Kool-Aid.

She worked in housing development so she knew about construction.

I ran to the bathroom so she wouldn't see me. My eyes were filled with pressure and soon nothing else would fit in them. I looked the medicine cabinet mirror with the chipped corner, brown with age.

Our house is little and dirty and it will always be.

It's my fault we're still living here.

I held on to the sink with both hands. *There's nothing wrong with our house.* I screamed in my head loud enough so that all of me could believe it. The littlest part still did not.

Rose and I had the same kinds of education: two bachelor's and two master's degrees. It didn't matter. It didn't matter that Rose had lived in dingy New York apartments smaller than my house. What mattered was that she was trying to help — isn't that the injury? If someone's trying to help you, that means you can't fix it yourself, and what's worse? She thought what she said was a compliment. I was shaking with anger. The afternoon light through the bathroom window was dimming. I couldn't hide for much longer.

I'd prayed that a cockroach would not run out between our feet as we stood in the living room. But then another kind of roach appeared out of the corner of my eye.

The truth was that my family was still living in the house — Amá, Dad, and my two brothers — not me. I had gotten out and lived in as close to a castle as I could. The thing that had slipped inside my stomach earlier had turned into guilt and stayed there.

When the pressure in my eyes subsided, I joined Rose and Amá outside. We drank dark red agua de Jamaica. It was tartly sweet, as if my heart were not bruised.

Amá made a joke with Rosita, as she called her. Rose's Spanish accent was a treat to Amá's ears.

"La Rosita tries so hard," Amá says. "Bien cute."

Rose and Amá were grinning at the other's cuteness standing underneath the room Amá built. Cute friends. Cute little plants. Cute.

When we got back to our flat, I went back to my old habit of inviting a select few to Amá's house. I kept that to lovers who would avoid what hurt me (and invited them only at the beginning of the love), and friends whose houses were also infested with poverty.

¤

I look up from where I'm writing this — bamboo trees and a blue sky and time to write — and I say, Fuck you, pobreza. Fuck you, whiteness, you pinche dinosaur that's always trying to help people who don't want it.

Yo soy una niña que estoy viendo un castillo.
Esta es su casita de Vickie.
There is nothing wrong with my house.

BRITTANY NEIMETH, *THE HOUSES, #2*, 2016, DIGITAL ARCHIVAL PRINT FROM MEDIUM FORMAT PHOTOGRAPH, 40 X 50 INCHES. WWW.BRITTANYNEIMETH.COM

SECOND LANGUAGE

PIOTR FLORCZYK

It's rained for so long
that I haven't left the couch
in days. Poets sprawl
across me, predicting
the world's end –
will it come with a bang
or tomatoes ripening on the vine?
Feeble-hearted Chopin
practices his funeral march
with "a small hand."
My next-door neighbors –
"Dinner time!" –
don't mind the rain
or that our initials
disappear from the curb.

After reading *Maus*
I look in the mirror and see
a pig made in Art's image.
Then I read it again,
backward, but the same
frayed speech bubbles
hover over my head.
The pit of smoldering
questions grows deeper.
Years ago, in Warsaw,
I went to see *that* heart –
stowed away inside
the first pillar on the left, it is
what keeps the world
from falling apart.

BEFORE AND AFTER

PIOTR FLORCZYK

Wind blows in from the North: a single-pane
shudders: filling this room my breath
forms into hedgehogs before my eyes.

If I didn't know any better I'd say the leafless
poplars across the street are shaking their hips for me.
But what do I know? Sometimes it's hard to tell

what's next, and next after that. If it's true
that beyond good and evil there's only more evil,
then I choose the now, i.e., my index finger

tapping on my scummed front teeth –
the hollow *tap-tap-tap* matching the first
drops of rains falling on the parapet.

Which reminds me of that day the weatherman
said, "A stray tropical storm will hang around
for days." D. and I went to work, inspecting the roof,

then built a tent with sheets and skis
in the attic, which we dubbed the great indoors.
We made ponchos out of Tyvek wrap.

We gave the retired pontoon that carried us
down the American the previous summer
one more mouth-to-mouth and it became our bed.

The Who's Who of Ellis Island tome kept
the door open at all times. By the time the guard
drove by in an armored ice-cream truck, announcing,

"The storm had fizzled out miles from LA,"
we'd already made a pact to live day-by-day
and stage our own May Parade, with the Stars

and Stripes trailing behind B-52s strung
from the rafters. "We shall defend our island."
Nobody saw us turn into snails carrying

each other's shells. "We shall fight
in the fields and in the streets, we shall fight
in the hills." We lasted a week, said the *Ledger*,

under "Immigrants and the Elements," but for once
we weren't embarrassed about who we were.
The fire chief made us promise we'd stop

carrying our stuff in plastic grocery bags,
with a proof of purchase, since we'll never be
allowed to exchange ourselves. That's how D. and I

became émigrés, first-time astronauts
surveying lost valleys of flesh, in our own house.
I hewed two-by-fours while she boiled the water

for stuffed cabbage rolls. "We shall fight
on the beaches, we shall fight on the landing grounds."
Alas, this feeling of having been everywhere

yet still needing to hit the road comes over me.
The signs have been there all along.
In the silent film uncoiling in my mind

I speed down country lanes. The slated-roof
barns are less the past than what might've been
had I not strayed off the path en route

to church. As luck would have it, the trail
I left became another. I roamed among trees,
scraping my ears on the bark. After two hours

I found a wheel rut that led me to the pond
and through a field of blueberries that made
my stomach growl. My juice-stained mouth

and *Iron Maiden* T-shirt didn't please the driver
inspecting his tanker at the Shell station.
After he saw me come out of the woods,

he scratched his head for a minute, then called me
a thief and punched me in the teeth. "We shall
never surrender." I remain a hunter-gatherer

who spends his time between dog-eared stamps
and coins that sweat when he gropes them.
Blame the 12-foot ceilings, with exposed

beams and wiring, for making me feel small.
The floorboards creak only when I tiptoe.
Rent is cheap so we put up with garbage heaps

outside our front door, or the torn screen that flaps
in the wind like cut-open skin. D. hates how restless
I get, aiming to track down every evil thought

I've had, sleeping three hours per night.
When my mind tires I start hammering in nails
and hanging pictures of a city lost in fog,

glowing like an anthill at dusk. Neighbors
know better than to ask why. The cracks
spread across the walls. Let it rain, D. says.

HALF-FULL OF GRACE

DOROTHY FORTENBERRY

"YOU DON'T HAVE to like it. You just have to go," I tell my five-year-old kid every Sunday when she complains about going to church. Every Sunday, even though she would prefer to stare at my phone, I make her go anyway.

Even though my phone is extremely wonderful.

Even though our religion — like all religions — has been responsible for terrible things.

Even though I often find the whole thing nutty and tacky, like a theme restaurant or the kind of museum you visit on a road trip.

Even though, when I was a kid and was similarly dragged by my mom, I was convinced — *convinced* — that I would never go again of my own free will.

Every Sunday, we go.

This is my attempt to explain why.

¤

> "If the concept of God has any validity or any use, it can only be to make us larger, freer, and more loving. If God cannot do this, then it is time we got rid of Him."
> — James Baldwin, *The Fire Next Time*

I live in Los Angeles. I am a screenwriter.

Being a screenwriter in Los Angeles is like being on a perpetual second date with everyone you know. You strive to be your most charming, delightful, quirky-but-not-damaged self because you never know what will come of the encounter. Maybe it's just a coffee. Maybe it's the coffee that leads to a job. Maybe it's the job that leads to a series. Maybe you'll get career-married and make career-babies. Who knows! So, you wear flattering jeans and an expensive, casual shirt, and you smile.

This is not such a bad life. Compared to other lives that I have lived, it is, frankly, an awesome one. I am very, very happy being a screenwriter in Los Angeles, particularly in the current age of Peak TV. It's a marvelous gig that I am grateful for.

But being on a perpetual second date can get exhausting. Constantly feeling that you should be meeting people, impressing people, shocking people (just the right amount) is a strange way to live your life. And one of the reasons that I go to church is that church is the opposite of that.

I do not impress anyone at church. I do not say anything surprising or charming, because the things I say are rote responses that someone else decided on centuries ago. I am not special at church, and this is the point. Because (according to the ridiculous, generous, imperfectly applied rules of my religion) we are all equally beloved children of God. We are all exactly the same amount of special. The things that I feel proud of can't help me here, and the things that I feel embarrassed by are beside the point. I'm a person but, for 60 minutes, I'm not a personality.

Another thing that I value: When I go to church in Los Angeles, I am a white person in a majority nonwhite space. In a city that's an oxymoronic 70 percent minority, that shouldn't be a special occurrence, but it is. Even more special is that I have come with no particular agenda. I have not come to teach or volunteer or try a new (to me) cuisine or inhabit a new (to me) neighborhood. I have not even come to act as an "ally." I have come to sit next to people, well aware of all we don't have in common, and face together in the same direction. Halfway through church, I turn to the congregants next to me and share the peace. I wish that they experience peace in their lives. That's it. They wish the same for me. Our words are identical. Our need for peace is infinite.

Church is a group of broken individuals united only by our brokenness traveling together to ask to be fixed. It's like a subway car. It's like the DMV. It's like *The Wizard of Oz*: we are each missing something, and there is a man in a flowing robe whom we trust to hand that something over.

(And I know — *I know* — that the problem with this metaphor is that, in *The Wizard of Oz*, there wasn't actually anyone with magical powers behind the curtain. I get it.)

But church is not just about how I feel or whom I'm surrounded by. It's about faith. This part is harder for me to explain.

¤

> "You pray for the hungry, then you feed them. That's how prayer works."
> — Pope Francis (at least, according to Pinterest)

I like being Catholic because long ago, people who were smarter than me and thought about it much longer than I have time to figured out what I'm supposed to believe. All I have to do is show up and recite a long list that starts with "I believe" and ends with the title of a Mountain Goats album. Whether I actually believe all the stuff about Jesus and Mary and Light from Light, true God from true God varies. Most of the time, I do, I think. Sometimes I don't. The single most annoying thing a nonreligious person can say, in my opinion, isn't that religion is oppressive or that religious people are brainwashed. It's the kind, patronizing way that nonreligious people have of saying, "You know, sometimes I *wish* I were religious. I *wish* I could have that certainty. It just seems so *comforting* never to doubt things."

Well, sometimes I wish I had the certainty of an atheist. I wish I could be positive that there was no God and that Sundays were for brunch. That dead people stayed dead and prayer was useless and Jesus was nothing more than a really great teacher.

But I believe too much, at least sometimes, to be certain about that. Sometimes I feel like I believe almost everything the church teaches and sometimes I feel like I believe almost nothing, but if I'm anywhere from one to 99 percent on the belief scale, my response is the same. If it's more than zero, I should go to church.

I do not find religion to be generally comforting in the way that I think nonreligious people mean it. I do not believe that everything in my life will necessarily be all right and I certainly do not believe that everything happens for a reason. I believe that whatever kind of God exists is the kind of God who can't or won't interfere every time humans decide to do horrible things to each other, because humans are clearly doing terrible things to each other every day and show very few signs of stopping.

It is not comforting to know quite as much as I do about how weaselly and weak-willed I am when it comes to being as generous as Jesus demands. Thanks to church, I have a much stronger sense of the sort of person I would like to be, and I am forced to confront all the ways in which I fail, daily. Nothing promotes self-awareness like turning down an opportunity to bring children to visit their incarcerated parents. Or avoiding shifts at the food bank. Or calculating just how much I will put in the collection basket. Thanks to church, I have looked deeply into my own heart and found it to be of merely small-to-medium size. None of this is particularly comforting.

Which is not to say there aren't parts of church that are comforting. It is comforting, for instance, to sing songs in a group. Singing alongside other people is a basic human pleasure that extends back across time and culture, and it's a shame to me that many adult Americans only experience it before baseball games. The songs that we sing in church are many of the same post-Vatican II songs I grew up singing. They sound like they should be on *Sesame Street* circa 1970, and I unabashedly adore them. It is comforting to loudly sing something that has little to no redeeming aesthetic value.

It is comforting to pray. Even without full knowledge or understanding of how the prayer will be received, it is comforting to offer up one's wishes for the world. In a time of stress and anxiety and distrust, it is comforting to be direct about what a possible alternative would look like. Someone leads the prayers every week at church and the kinds of things we pray for are both straightforward (an end to the death penalty; a living wage for all workers; safe homes for refugees; care for the planet and its climate) and very difficult to achieve, which makes them ideal subjects for prayer.

When I think about any of these things outside of church, my blood pressure skyrockets and I go into a mild panic attack. When I pray about them in church, I feel like I am doing a tiny bit to help.

Thought about with even a smidgen of rationality, prayer makes no sense. If you asked me point blank what I believe about how God picks and chooses among petitions ranging from new sneakers to the stopping of genocide, I would stammer incoherently. I would tell you, I suppose, that God has some sort of triage system that I can't figure out, but also that anyone who wants to should pray for anything they want — why not? It seems presumptuous to self-censor our prayers for fear they are not worthy of His time. If anyone is able to structure His time efficiently, it ought to be God.

I would also tell you that, when facing a medical difficulty in one of my pregnancies to which doctors responded, "wait and see," I asked the priest at church to put his hands on my belly and pray. I would tell you that my best friend asked her church in Indiana to pray for my pregnancy, too, and the thought of a bunch of people sending their wishes for my potential child into the air still moves me more than I know what to do with.

I don't know if the feeling I get when I think about this is God.

I do know that I want it to be.

¤

"We say
pinhole.
A pin hole
of light. We
can't imagine
how bright
more of it
could be,
the way
this much
defeats night.
It almost
isn't fair,
whoever
poked this,
with such
a small act
to vanquish
blackness."
— Kay Ryan, "Pinhole"

Church isn't an escape from the world. It's a continuation of it. My family and I don't go to church to deny the existence of the darkness. We to go to look so hard at the light that our eyes water.

❖

KIM TRUONG, *DEPART II*, 2010, PORCELAIN, DIMENSIONS BETWEEN 5 AND 20 INCHES. PHOTO: MICHAEL UNDERWOOD

REQUIEM FOR A REQUIEM

CAROL MUSKE-DUKES

Requiem for a Requiem
– Paula Modersohn-Becker, 1876–1907

In art, she reminds us, one is alone with oneself.
Familiar mantra she repeats to keep her self
intent on those tentative strokes, till the brush

splays hard-flat against the canvas. *Women*
aren't meant to paint other women naked. Women
aren't meant to attack the canvas. She turns out still

lifes, loyal grapes, a spite-green goblet, sun-lit.
Fruit, sexualized. Goldblack nipples, mons veneris.
Women standing naked right there in no-one's gaze.

Women nursing unclothed, dreaming faces un-
readable above the urgent mouth. First to offer
the female body unburdened by notions of pose. First

to haunt *him*: perpetually self-haunted Rilke, from
beyond her own self-predicted grave, after first
seeing her daughter's face. Still she walks the fields

near Worpswede, then angles the brush beam-high
to gauge a laughing face, off-kilter. Open doorway,
somebody's wife. She's seen Cezanne's oranges,

pre-Cubist Picassos in Paris. She knows what they know.
Drifting in spirit material through Rilke's "Requiem."
Summoned in her once-body, back-lit as in a self-portrait,

clothed only in *Das Ding*, the thing in itself. He beckons
her into candlelight, but she turns away. Something makes
her pause, listen: is it the startled sound of her own final

breath, unpent at the end? Or caught quick at the start,
her death writ at the instant she gives her body over to
it: the chance-implacable site of conception, where some

(even now) insist is the point at which all life begins.

WRITERS WHO BRUNCH:

Getting the Dish from Scribes Doing Double-Duty in Publishing and TV

JANICE RHOSHALLE LITTLEJOHN

WITH A GROWING number of books being adapted to series, it's a wonder there aren't more novelists writing for television. In reality, while that might sound glamourous, writing in both mediums is not for the faint of heart, as I learned over a Sunday morning brunch roundtable with Los Angeles novelist and TV writer Leonard Chang; novelist and supervising producer of *Empire*, Attica Locke; and young adult novelist and TV writer Jen Klein.

¤

JANICE RHOSHALLE LITTLEJOHN: *Did you intend to have this kind of multi-hyphenated writing career when you were starting out?*

ATTICA LOCKE: There was nothing intentional about it for me. I started off as a feature writer. I was a feature writer for well over a decade. But nothing ever got made. I felt like all I did was drive around to meetings. I was writing to get to the next meeting. So I walked away from all of it and decided to write a book. That turned into writing three books, and I thought, "This is my new career." But the financials of book writing are a challenge — especially if you have a kid in private school and live in L.A.

So I was thinking of other revenue streams, and TV, during the time I was writing books, was getting really interesting. I was able to see the parallels between book writing and the incredibly novelistic TV we're all watching, with its deep character work. It's all the stuff that I had been trying to do as a feature writer — but they don't make those movies anymore, like grown-up-people stuff. So I reached out to try my hand at that, and then landed the job of a lifetime, which was *Empire* [on Fox].

JEN KLEIN: I was also trying the feature track, and all the meetings … it was so hard. And I realized when I'm at home at night, I don't want to watch a movie, I want to watch TV. I want to go on a long, long, long journey. I don't know why I never thought before then that I wanted to write for it. I think the hours or the work, the way you're so invested, seemed daunting. My kids were smaller, and books were another thing to try. I found out I loved writing books at the same time I started pursuing TV, and I loved them both so much that I didn't want to give up either one for the other. So now I'm at *Grey's* — *Grey's Anatomy* [on ABC] — and I cannot express how much I love it there. And I'm also writing books.

LEONARD CHANG: I always wanted to write novels. I wrote my first novel [unpublished], when I was in high school, and after a bit of a circuitous path of traveling in the Peace Corps, I decided to hunker down and write more. I went to grad school and started publishing novels in my 20s, and then — very similar to [Attica] — I began seeing things on TV that were really blowing me away, tackling crime and family and social issues on a very broad canvas, with a lot of insight and depth. It was basically *The Wire.*

I'd published my sixth novel, and I decided I needed to try to do both, so I moved down to L.A. from the Bay Area, and began trying to sell shows. I needed to learn more about the producorial aspect so I began staffing, and was staffed on *Awake* [on NBC] and on *Justified* [FX]. Now I'm on *Snowfall* [John Singleton's 1980's cocaine-epidemic drama pilot for FX] and still trying to create and sell my own stuff.

Have you adapted any of your novels for screen?

CHANG: I've adapted *Dispatches from the Cold* (1998) and *Over the Shoulder* (2001) for various feature production companies, but neither got made. I'm currently working on an adaptation of *Over the Shoulder* meant for a cable TV series. I'm very interested in adapting all my work for TV in the future.

KLEIN: My books have not yet been adapted for screen. I've definitely considered adapting them in the future — possibly when I have a second to breathe in between *Grey's* and book deadlines. I've always been able to see *Jillian Cade* as a series, and I love the idea of *Shuffle, Repeat* as a feature. But I have not pursued either of those — yet.

LOCKE: *Black Water Rising* (2009) is the only book that's been optioned. I was approached about doing a draft of the screenplay, but the timing wasn't right. I was finishing up its sequel, *Pleasantville* (2015), and didn't think I could write the character, Jay Porter, at two different ages at the same time — and I was also starting work on *Empire*. I'd like to do an adaptation of my work one day, but I could live with someone else doing it — if they do it well.

Novel writing comes from a singular voice. TV writing is collaborative. How are you each able to find your voice on a series among a team of television writers?

KLEIN: As far as voice goes, I started in season 11 on *Grey's Anatomy,* so there was voice for miles when I came in, and the challenge was being able to write in that voice. But my voice still comes out in the stories I contribute, pitching in the room. It's not always what you say in the room that shows up on the screen, but something that you said contributed.

CHANG: I've been lucky to work on shows where the amalgamation of the voices is very enjoyable. And what's been wonderful about TV is that it is a highly collaborative medium, and so even if my voice isn't particularly coinciding with the group voice, my voice participates and helps form that group voice, and there's a respect for my participation and my contribution. It's a nice change of pace to go from staying in your room all alone for 10 hours, seven days a week, to being in a room with very intelligent, like-minded, skilled storytellers.

LOCKE: From the very beginning, I do remember walking into the room wondering, "How in the world does this all work?" And then after a couple of weeks into season one, I got the idea of the groupthink. I'm finding my bigger challenge now. When I first started *Empire*, my third book was written. I'm presently writing my first book while being on the show — and that is not fun. I actually said to myself, "I'm not even sure I want to do this again." I'm having a problem not trusting my instincts as strongly because I live in a culture where everything's done by committee. Whatever I put on page, I'm like, "Is that okay?" Nobody else is telling me. There's a part of me that misses being alone and doing one thing for months at a time, because I like that long journey, and I like the idea of singularly. So I wouldn't have it any other way, because I don't want to lose books.

Who inspires you as a writer?

KLEIN: I read voraciously as a child and I was shy, as probably a lot of us writers were, just reading constantly. My parents had a giant collection of the classics, and they all had that sort of old paper smell. I used to read all of them as a kid way before I understood them. It's that thing where you read *Frankenstein* in high school and go, "Oh, that's what that was about. It wasn't just a monster." So I grew up on all that. TV these days, there's so much good stuff and stories you couldn't tell five years ago, 10 years ago. Look at *Transparent.* [Jill Soloway's] amazing. I am inspired every day by what continues to be made and what continues to be watched on a regular basis.

LOCKE: Dennis Lehane [*Gone, Baby, Gone* [1998)] is a kinda sorta a mentor of mine. He published my second book [*The Cutting Season* (2012)] — he has a small imprint at HarperCollins. I would go so far as to say we're friends. We've had lunch together. We've done a writers festival together. But I feel shy to call him up, 'cause I still see myself as a fan of his. Even though I know personally he's a fan of mine. I've wanted to talk to him about *The Drop* (2014), which was his little novella and is now a movie, and he also wrote the script for the movie. He's gone from these procedural-esque series things — he's done *Mystic River* (2001), *Shutter Island* (2003) — then made that shift and has done these grand historical epics like *The Given Day* (2008), and *The Drop* is like this little 230-page somethin'. I'm trying to write a slimmer book than I normally write, and I wanted to ask him: "How did you switch?" How do you, in a lifetime, write both The Given Day and this 230-page novella?

CHANG: For me, in terms of novels, when I first started out, I was really enamored with the modernists — the Hemingway-Fitzgerald-Faulkner of it all. But as I grew into my own voice as a writer and began writing more about issues of race and family, certain authors like James Baldwin and Ernest Gaines began to resonate, and they are still my paragons. When I moved to television and film, there are certain voices like David Simon, or certain shows like *The Sopranos,* that hit different angles of what I was interested in, and in trying to demarcate the different worlds, it took a while for me to do both at the same time. What I found is that I have to flip a switch in my head, and so in the early mornings, I'm in novelist mode, and by 10 o'clock you can flip a switch, and now you're in TV mode.

How do you balance your writing lives?

LOCKE: During the week, I pledge myself to *Empire.* If I can come home and squeeze in a little something else, fine. But it's basically my kid and *Empire.* On the weekends at home, I write in bed. I don't normally write in bed, but for this particular book, that is my office.

CHANG: My schedule is very vigorous, and it has been for many years. I get up at four or five in the morning, and I'm usually in the office by six. That's when I do most of my own writing — and some of the show writing, like dailies and stuff. By 10, the room is starting up, and I work all day in the room until about six, and I'll work in the office for another hour or two. Then I go home, do all the home stuff, bills. Then go to bed relatively early and that's usually it. On the weekends, I'll spend more time on my own work, but I still have to do some stuff on the show, and generally the hours aren't as long, but I do work weekends. I've been doing that schedule for about seven or eight years.

LOCKE: Just so I don't feel bad, you don't have a child, right?

CHANG: No child. There's no way I could work like this if I had a child.

KLEIN: I didn't know what vast amounts of time I had until I had my first child, and it was all gone. Everything went to this baby, and then another baby, and then I look back and think, "What was I doing in my early 20s? I could have written 15 books."

My craziest time last year while at *Grey's*, I signed a contract for two books — my third and fourth — and they wanted book number three to come out at the same time as the paperback for number two. So because of that, the publishers gave me this compressed schedule that I — apparently I still think I need to say "yes" to everything — agreed to, and had to write it in, like, three months post outline. In that time, I was also scheduled to write an episode of *Grey's* [season 12, episode 18].

From December to March, I would get up in the morning, shower, grab food, go to the office, and work there. At home, I was helping with the kids and getting them ready for school, so I would go to the office and work there for two or three hours until 10 o'clock and then brain switch over to *Grey's Anatomy*. Then go home, say hello to my husband, kiss my kids, grab food, go to the home office, and work there.

LOCKE: I'm living a version of that, although I've already asked for an extension on my deadline. I'm supposed to have a book due in September [2016] — that's never gonna happen. [Laughter.] Our production is in Chicago, so when we have episodes we then fly there [writers produce their own episodes]. So I'm in another city, and I have to be on-set while writing another episode, while I'll be writing the next one with a book helicoptering over all of it. But as much as my heart is racing talking about this, I also feel that sense of kinship talking to you guys — this is doable.

KLEIN: Mine's not out yet, so we'll see. [Laughter.] It might not be.

There is a meme on social media describing a writing career as "having homework for the rest of your life." How do you sum up your writing life?

CHANG: I can barely remember a time when I haven't written — it's almost a part of thinking for me. I can actually process the world better when I'm writing, and the world that I'm living in infuses the writing, and so I can't imagine not writing. When people talk about writing in terms of schedules, or homework, or assignments, it's a different approach for me. It's how I live.

KLEIN: I start to get cuckoo if I'm not writing. If I'm between something and haven't figured out what the next project is, I start to become a little bananas. It's what keeps me level headed, having a place to put all of that.

LOCKE: It is the price of admission: to wake up thinking about something; to go to bed thinking about it; to be in line at the grocery store, opening my notes app when I think of something so I can jot it down. We talk about writing schedules, and that's the scheduling of it. But even in the times that you're not at the desk, you're still constantly thinking of it. It's just a life.

We're seeing more people of color on TV, but the statics regarding women and people of color in writing, producing, and directing positions is stagnant. What is impeding increased diversity behind-the-scenes?

CHANG: It's an issue of expediency and laziness. You have a television show that's basically a $200-million company, and when the people at the top are hiring, they're very, very scared of screwing up a $200-million company, and they choose the people they're most familiar with, people they've worked with before, the people that have been vetted by the studios and networks — and those, for many, many years, have basically been white men.

It's only lately that there's been more pressure, and more awareness and sensitivity, on the question of exclusion, and now it takes a certain amount of energy and effort to say, "Okay, I'm going to take a chance on someone I haven't worked with before, and give this person a chance." So it's a matter of a slow and steady and pervasive effort to convince everyone at the top that it's going to be okay. In fact, it's going to be better than before, and it can make a lot of money. That shift only started happening, from my perspective, within the past five years.

There's a similar shift in books. When I first started writing books about Asian-American and African-American characters, it was very much a similar sort of aesthetic: "We, the publishers, expect to see a certain kind of character and if you don't fulfill our expectations, we're not interested." It's that same stubbornness and inability to see beyond what they're familiar with, and that's just going to take time and people in the trenches to keep pushing.

LOCKE: One of the things I really respect about my boss on *Empire*, Ilene Chaikin, is that not only has she made a point, obviously, to fill the [writer's] room with people of color and with women, but she has made a clear point to have as many women as possible directing the show. She's using the success of the show. Who's going to question what Ilene is doing? Ilene made this huge hit. She's using that power in a really great way.

KLEIN: All of us who have been in these situations and go, "This is how I can help to make a change." I've seen that this change works and is the right thing to do.

But would any of you have had these opportunities if you weren't novelists with certain storytelling skillsets that could be transferred to screen?

LOCKE: When I went to meet on *Empire*, nobody counted me being a novelist as a knock against me. They were just curious, "What is that?" At least I had some credits before I started all of this, then nothing for years except writing books. In other meetings, people would say, "What the hell have you been doing for years?" The book thing didn't mean anything. But Lee Daniels had never worked in TV. Danny Strong had never worked in [series] TV, so *Empire*, from jump, never felt like we were doing this the regular way. So I got lucky to walk into a run with people who were curious about what, as a novelist, I might bring to the room.

CHANG: When you are up against the 23-year-old from USC, and you walk into a room and they're trying to break stories about life, I come in and say, "I'm older, I've written about this stuff — hundreds of pages of this stuff." Then someone can go, "Maybe you can be helpful." That's the key: where can you bring something to the table? Spending years on a book, researching it, and understanding long narratives, is incredibly important now, especially in serialized TV. You're not just looking for one episode, you're looking for 10, 13, 22 episodes over five or six years. Those skills come in handy.

KLEIN: And they know you can work alone. They know you have the ability to go off and write your script in your little writer cave — alone. [Laughter.] Some people look at it as a depth that you're bringing to the table. Being a novelist comes with this perceived extra gold dust on it.

❖

AMITA BHATT, *A FANTASTIC COLLISION OF THE THREE WORLDS-XXII*, 2013, CHARCOAL AND OIL STICK ON CANVAS, 9 X 12 FEET ©AMITA BHATT

LAWS OF ANNIHILATION

ERIQ LA SALLE

PROLOGUE

GOD HAD SURELY outdone Himself. The bucolic hamlet of Eagle Hill, New York, was only two hours north of Manhattan but it felt much more like a different era entirely. From the natural springs and rolling hills to the never-ending vistas it was immediately clear why the Iroquois who were the first to settle there called it "The land of a thousand wonders." There were at least thirty shades of green from the various species of trees and groundcover outlining the handful of horse ranches and farms. The place had big yards and the type of affordable acreage that made a man feel richer than he was. With its population of just under two thousand, the locals dubbed their quaint existence "Heaven by the Hudson."

It was a beautiful Fourth of July and families came from as far away as Pennsylvania, Connecticut, and Delaware, as well as the five boroughs of New York. They came for the annual Heritage Pride Picnic, which was sponsored by Ellis Brock, a wealthy Wall Street trader turned evangelical preacher. He owned forty acres of good earth and privacy. The event was originally a family reunion but quickly grew in size each year. It was by invitation only and not even the locals were allowed to attend.

Ellis Brock loved the peals of children's laughter echoing through the valley. He stood by and took it all in: the chasing, the catching, the tumbling down hills that were made for such oft forgotten joys. There was kickball, apple-bobbing, face-painting and even sack races. Parents actually took delight in the grass stains and dirt that covered their children's clothing. Fathers manned the grills as mothers piled plates high with smoked ribs, pork links and barbecue chicken with potato salad and corn on the cob. It took two picnic tables to hold all of the cakes, pies and numerous other sweets. The event was a throwback to more innocent times—an environment where kids spent the day without a worry in the world. No video games or phones or computers of any kind were allowed; not even cameras. The kids used their imaginations to entertain themselves and the parents used the time as a reminder of sweeter days.

Shortly after sunset Brock stood on a raised platform under a banner that read "THE ALLIANCE FOR A BETTER TOMORROW" and addressed the nearly two hundred people in attendance. He was a tall man in his late fifties and carried with him a certain regality; not the kind that one is born with but rather the kind that has been practiced for years. He had a thick nest of snow-white hair that was a random mix of perfect curls and intersecting waves. He had sea-blue eyes and his pigmentation was as pale as baby powder. Ellis Brock was a rather imposing albino. The crowd grew silent as he took the stage. From the youngest to the oldest, all eyes were on him. When Brock spoke, everyone listened.

> "I love this great country. My country. My father's country and his father before him. Know your history people. Our ancestors cultivated this land and developed the technology and created a nation of greatness. And each time the welfare of this nation was threatened did we not rise to its defense? From the Civil War to the Gulf Wars we are a people who rise to the defense of our nation. Well I stand before you this evening to tell you that our glorious nation is in peril. Threatened with inevitable destruction. Destruction of the values and the morals that have become the very fiber of our existence. Destruction of our land and of our homes and of our dreams and of our future. Destruction of the dreams and the future of our children and our children's children's children. The greatest nation in the world and we turn our backs on our farmers. We foreclose on the homes of our mothers and fathers. We steal the jobs from our most qualified. We undermine the potential of our best and our brightest. We…no, not we…them. The hypocritical liberal. The puppet politicians. The soulless Jew. The amoral nigger. The parasitic immigrant and all the other innumerable undesirables that have infested this land. These days they say it's not considered politically correct to denounce another group of people. Well I'm here today to tell you that if being pro-Christian means that I'm anti-Semitic, then so be it. If being pro-white is anti-nigger, then so be it. In times of war political correctness is an ineffective weapon. Don't be fooled people these are most certainly times of war. We are God's chosen. Blessed soldiers for the Lord. They may call us many things but if we are truly going to make this country great again then the only title we need concern ourselves with being worthy of is the title of American. God Bless America!"

All those assembled cheered their charismatic hero. Even though the small children had no true comprehension of the content of Brock's speech they followed the lead of their parents and clapped enthusiastically. As Brock stepped down off the platform to a warm reception, bluegrass music began to play. For the next two hours the night air was filled with merriment. They danced. They laughed. They ate and drank all that they could. As much as Eagle Hill was an idyllic wonderland in the daylight, it was absolutely breathtaking at night. It was a place where there were far more stars than sky. The dull, silver moon dangled from heaven like loose change in God's pocket. Fireworks lit up the patches of black sky. It was all so very perfect. And still there was more entertainment to come.

The main attraction started promptly at ten. Three large men led a hooded man with his hands tied behind his back out of a barn. The burlap sack that covered his head was soaked in a couple of areas with dark, red spots that shimmered like silk under the light of the moon. Each time the man slowed he was struck across his buttocks with an oak two-by-four as though he were an uncooperative field mule. The dancing stopped and the band stopped playing. The crowd followed the foursome to the northwest corner of the property. There they assembled around a giant red oak that was at least two hundred years old. Its lowest branch was twelve feet high and a foot and a half in diameter. It was a good hanging tree. As the man's hood was removed the crowd jeered at the black man that stood trembling before them. Both of his eyes were swollen and fresh streaks of blood looked painted beneath his nose, mouth and ears. Not that it would have done much good but he was unable to scream for help because his tongue had been burned useless with a branding iron. The coarse rope that was tightened around his neck scraped his skin like rolled sandpaper. Some in the crowd frowned as though they were personally offended that the man defecated on himself as he was hoisted off of his feet. As the heavy set man was suspended six feet in the air with his legs violently kicking for life not a single man woman or child turned away. Some of the younger children even giggled at the funny black man dancing on air. Ellis Brock beaming with pride stood front and center with his wife on one side of him and his eight year-old son, Ellis Brock Jr. to his left. When the hanging man's neck snapped Brock Jr. flinched and tried to turn away. Brock Sr. turned his son's head back toward the swinging corpse. Even though the sight of the dead man sickened the young boy, he forced himself to watch because he wanted nothing more than to be worthy of his father's pride. He stared at the large oak and tried looking past the dangling strange fruit it bore. Ellis Brock Sr. rested his hand on his son's shoulder proud not just by the day's events but buoyed by the fact that he was surrounded by hard working, faithful Christians that shared his vision of how great America could be once again.

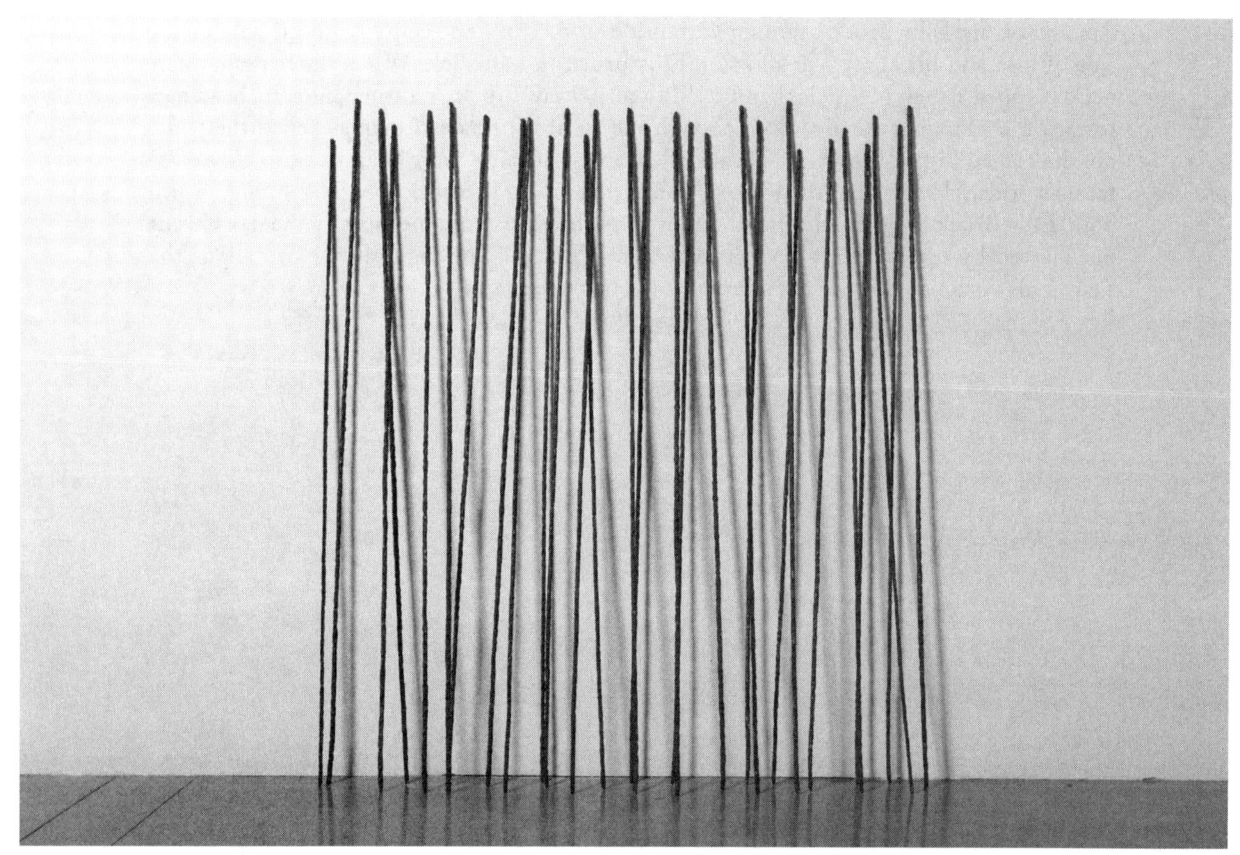

KIM TRUONG, *STICKS*, 2014, FIRED CLAY, GLAZES, DIMENSIONS BETWEEN 64 AND 70 INCHES. PHOTO: MARTYNA NIESZCZESNA

BELLE

THELMA T. REYNA

Her left eye droops, eyelashes twitching, ever since it healed three years ago. Used to be a matching set, large hazel eyes, Mila Kunis eyes, one skewed left now with the broken nose between.

She sweeps eyeliner, iridescent shadow on her puckered lids, peering in the mirror where the glass is still intact. The largest shard sliced chin and ear last year when he slammed her face into its frame.

Georgia Belle, they called her once, and draped the sash across her chest. Folks love beauty queens, the emcee said, and the photo on her restroom wall, crown and all, proves her looks were once intact.

She dabs rouge on sunken cheeks, one lower with pummeled bones when he jumped bail last summer and sneaked home. Tonight she checks locks, steps out with friends, and doesn't know when he'll be back again.

SHORT FOR PENELOPE

LIBBY FLORES

"My job is to draw what I see, not what I know."
— J. M. W. Turner on why his painted ships had no portholes.

ON SUMMER AFTERNOONS, Penny would waste her time watching me doze off after sex. Poor kid, I have turned into a useless lover. I have a wife, and I have Penny. This year I'll have to share Thanksgiving with both of them. Pass the gravy?

Penny is my wife's goddaughter. She is short, with long, black hair. She twists her mouth to the left when she speaks. Dark hair and light eyes have always plagued me. She has perfect knees, small as elbows. She's just turned 23 — clearly old enough to know how to leave someone. Penny works at a coffee shop and paints, though she doesn't call herself an artist. She hasn't passed into that phase of impudence yet. I can drive to her apartment at any hour; she'll let me in and fix me a drink. I've been seeing her for a year. All her canvases face the wall. She says she won't let me see them — not good enough. She'd be better off fucking an artist than an English professor. Paint stains on her olive hands, she looks the part, her hair usually in some mess on top of her head. She always seems like she's right in the middle of something even if I've called ahead.

She loves J. M. W. Turner. I had the pleasure of taking her to see her first one — *Modern Rome — Campo Vaccino*. She welled up, stared down at her splattered Converse, and didn't speak the whole ride home. Later she said she didn't want to sleep with me anymore, that seeing something like that makes everything "much sadder." I think what she meant was — great art can upset your life, it can make you want to throw everything out and start over. I received zero credit for bringing her there. Just a glass of tap shoved in my direction and then a door in my face. She might've patted me on the back. Terrific getting to know you kid — you're a real people person.

Beth is the kind of woman you marry. A good redhead with a high IQ. She never wants me to open anything for her, not pickle jars, not car doors. She'd rather know her own strength. The lady likes cooking, a bleached countertop, and humming. She has hummed through most of our marriage. Tunes that have no end, that sound like songs, but are really defeated melodies. She is steady, calm, and the kind of reliable that goes without notice.

Godchildren are inherited. Beth just came to the church and watched her get dipped, that's all. A little holy water on Penny's head. I wasn't there. At that point in my life I avoided most ceremonies. Penny's mom, Beth's best friend, was just a kid herself. A kid with Catholic parents. All I remember is that was the week Beth told me she was pregnant. We were married a year later.

When Penny called, Beth hadn't seen her in quite some time. Then, two years ago, there she was at our dinner table after her father had his heart attack. A miserable drunk with a bum ticker. Penny is fatherless now. I don't do anything too kind for her or buy her things. I only take items over to her apartment that I need, like bourbon and toothpaste.

Beth brings in most of the money now. She came into a substantial inheritance. She also just published a cookbook about a healthy diet. Thirty ways to eat quinoa —quinoa brownies, quinoa salad, quinoa meatloaf — I ate it for weeks. Christ, my beard is made of it. She's getting a bit of press. It's hard to watch her on conference calls in our kitchen while I microwave leftovers. Enjoy it, B. All this attention will pass, and then you can tell them that whipped cream is really your favorite dish. She has no idea how hard her success is on me. I love her still, but we haven't had an interesting conversation in 10 years. I started a list when we first got married of all the things I love about her, one word adjectives. Every year on our anniversary I intend to give it to her, but then I want to add something, so I don't. Recently I have started another list. It goes the other way.

Four years ago our son Sam, who is grown now, set off homemade fireworks at his high school. It was more like a bomb; he injured a teacher and killed a student. Beth has never recovered. The boy looks taken from, although as an only child, he's never had to ask for a thing. I don't know why I think of this, but the student who died was wearing a green nylon parka. He was charred like a marshmallow, trying to save a girl from the blast. After being detained, Sam came home with a pen in his pocket; he's kept it on his desk for years. It was nothing special, a blue Bic, but it was melted and warped. I guess it was the boy's. But this is not about returning things.

Sam went to a Midwestern college. He got off with a misdemeanor: the court ruled that not only was he a minor, there was no intent to kill. But it's ruined his hopes of becoming a chemist. Now he's a business major and says he wants to marry rich.

The Catholics have it right. You just add it all up, say it in a box, and repent for an afternoon. Maybe you still feel guilty, but you know what to do with it. All this holding on makes you tired. It makes you want to go to some kid's house, let the parents open the door, and say *here's your fucking pen.*

Beth tore a ligament last week on the elliptical and is worried that she'll miss her New York *engagement.* A word she used to never say. Now that she's published this cookbook she thinks she has to be the picture of fitness. It won't last. Once Penny called me when Beth was home. I yelled into the phone, *Don't waste your time. We vote Republican in this house.* Beth laughed. No chance she'll ever call back now. I think of her with men her own age, but I'm not sure a young man could give her what she's after. She needs to feel like a discovery. Being raised with great inadvertency leads to a lifetime of yearning. The worst thing you can do to a girl like that is forget her.

Beth leaves me to work for long stretches of time in my office. There are women at the university nearby who like to jog up our road; once a day I find myself by my picture window, waiting for shorts and the brilliance of white cotton.

We are living in California, below the hills, not too far from the ocean, where no one remarks on the weather. There is research to be done. The deadline for my book, *First Impressions: The Poetics of Jane Austen,* is near. I'm revising a draft. There are a few friends who might actually care about this. I wish I still knew them.

I liked teaching at first — everything but the grading. You have to be a little romantic to push literature on the young. I've never slept with a student. When you teach undergrads you find that chasm between you and them. The girl with great legs you would've noticed at the grocery store becomes the one who's late, always chews gum, and talks over you. If you have a teenager at home, which I did, it's hard to see the difference. I guess Sam helped me to be faithful for a time. This is not to say I wasn't interested in some, or that the few who had read my books wouldn't find me in my office hours and say so. Sometimes they asked me to go for a drink, but I never went. I never wore my ring; Beth didn't care. She knows I hate jewelry and things you have to keep track of. There was a span of years where my colleagues also thought I was unmarried, because I never mentioned Beth, and if there was some party or function I went alone. She wasn't a showpiece and I didn't want to subject her to browning lettuce, bad wine, and worse conversations. I would find a way to never say her name. The truth was I hid her. I wanted to be autonomous. Penny changed that.

When you are only allowed a limited time to see someone everything seems paramount. The notion that I could take her somewhere and hold my hand at the small of her back was thrilling. Not to go to far-off deserted diners in the Valley at 4:00 p.m., not to make her sit in the car while I grabbed us Italian. To have actually dined out — that would've helped. You recognize the freedom that other couples have. You envy it. I got tired of suggesting obscure places. We'd usually end up at her apartment.

When I took her to the museum that day we toured the exhibit separately. I read the gallery labels, one of my favorite things to do at the Getty. I watched her from a distance as she stopped at each of the paintings, her regal head tilted up.

While I'm filling an ice pack for Beth, she yells from the couch, "Hey, I invited Penelope for Thanksgiving. I think she's alone this year." I keep breaking ice with a steak knife. "That means you'll need to get the extra leaf out of the garage."

It's nice that after years she finally needs me to help her. Of course Penny's alone; she prides herself on not having a boyfriend. I didn't think she'd come because of the way she left things, but now it's confirmed. I almost hit my thumb on the last stab.

Sam is coming too. He doesn't visit that often, and when he does, he spends a lot of time out of the house. I thought for a moment he was seeing someone here. We have kept his room just as he left it. Beth is sentimental about the boy's things.

I went in recently to find a reference book I remember loaning him for a term paper. I noticed that the warped pen was not on his desk. There were only a few reminders of his chemist past. A few dusty, glass apothecary funnels and beakers were balanced at the end of his bookshelf, and by his bed where most boys would hang a swimsuit centerfold was a periodic table of elements poster curling at its edges. The squares of color now faded from the direct sunlight. What used to be a row of bright orange noble gases had now turned the color of Beth's baked salmon. After the accident she was going to remove the poster as if it were some sort of foreshadowing we missed. She was frightened of him, maybe of the idea that the same small, tender hands that pushed down a cookie cutter to make gingerbread men at Christmas, years later built (quite possibly in this room) a deathly Cherry Bomb. But the poster had stayed, I think, because it was the last of his childhood things. He had outgrown the rest. He'd also held on to three Star Wars figures, and they seemed to watch me as I rifled through his desk drawers. I lost myself for a moment looking for that Bic, and after a few minutes I just walked out of his room, without the book I had come in to find. What was I going to do with that sad artifact?

When I told Penny about the accident she said she already knew. Of course she did, but I'd often like to think of her as some girl that had just wandered into town. It was not something I regularly discussed with people. We were in her bed and her hair looked even darker on the pillow. She said, "It is incredibly awful how one mistake can alter your life forever. He was just a stupid kid trying to show off."

It was moments like these that made her seem less like a twentysomething-year-old secret, and more like a second wife. Beth didn't like to talk about the accident — she's built on forward momentum. She probably doesn't know the pen exists. My eyes started to water at the words "stupid kid" so I gulped them down, and reached across Penny for my glass of whiskey.

I caught Sam creeping in one night last Christmas. He was quietly slipping off his beaten topsiders by the door. I was downstairs watching TV, eating what was left of the Rocky Road — Beth thinks she hides it behind the frozen peas. Sam flushed at the sight of me. His rusty, red hair had grown longer and was starting to curl like his mom's. When he comes home from college I catch a glimpse of the man he's becoming. It happens the instant I see him by the baggage carousel. He seems to gain an inch on me every six months. His suitcase looks smaller each time. That night I got a quick *Hi Dad*, then he escaped upstairs.

I would like him to have everything he wants. This is a feeling I've never had for anyone. He's done well at school. I knew the dean there, so his record was buried. The last time we spoke he said he might be bringing a girl home. "She's taller than me." I didn't like this picture so I asked, "What's her major?" He told me it was marine biology, which made me wonder why the hell she was out there. A Miami-born girl travels to Michigan State University to study marine biology? What was *she* trying to hide? Sam is terrible on the phone. There's always silence and the 15 minutes he gives me is just me asking questions, and him firing out fragments. *Not too bad. It's all right. Yeah Dad, I know.*

I had to deliver the news to him that the boy with the green jacket died. Beth was in pieces on a plastic chair in the hallway of the juvenile holding center. The police officer said he would tell him, but that's not the kind of thing you let a stranger do. Now I see in Sam's eyes that my face will be forever tied with that day, with what I thought was a decent deed.

Penny was always fond of me at holiday dinners. I always attempted a joke when things got pretentious. *Pass the ham* was usually followed by some eye contact. When she showed up last year she was a woman, no longer afraid to wear a low neckline. When she was younger she and Beth spent a lot of time on the phone. They got close because Penny's own mother was grieving. I never saw her during that time. But, at that dinner last year, she swore, put a napkin in her lap, and made bold statements about modern art while, unknowingly, she had red lipstick on her teeth. She sounded like an old film star who'd had too much to drink. Sam laughed at her in all the wrong places, and when Beth collected the plates she gave *me* a look. As if I'd done something. When Penny called the house the next day, it was to speak to me.

The first time I went to her place she learned my parents had died a few years apart when I was around her age. I think it was one of the reasons she slept with me. Also, I used the word *syncopation* while describing the beat of her dripping faucet. The items in her studio apartment were what my mother would've called *dear*. They were all chosen for show.

She had a shelf of china plates with hand-painted flowers around the edges. She served me a beer in a frosted mason jar. The only things not precious were those drying canvases facing the wall. They didn't seem cared for.

I know it's more than Older Man Fucks Pretty Girl. It's like someone opening your casket, and you pop up wide awake and you think, thank God, thank *Christ*, you came.

Penny prefers her nickname, but Beth never calls her that. Something about saying Penelope makes the godmother stuff official. Penny hasn't phoned since the museum. Every day something comes up that I want to tell her, but I've decided it's her turn to try and reach me. I still think of the way she throws her bras across the room when she gets undressed, as if she cares for nothing — blithely. Once I fished one out of her sink when I was washing a glass for bourbon. I've started a list for her, too.

Thanksgiving looms like a noose. This will be the first time I'll be in a room with both of them since I started the thing with Penny. Beth has ordered most of the dinner to be cooked and delivered by a well-known chef — big fan of her book. It seems extravagant, but I'm not paying for it.

I'm in my study rereading *Austen: A Life*. This is something I do when I can't write. It never does much for my mood. When we moved in, Beth gave me one of the best rooms in the house for my office. We chose a midcentury place — clean lines, lots of glass. I can hear the sound of pans being pulled out of the cupboard when I come downstairs. Beth is in the kitchen, on a stool, mixing something in a bowl. Without raising her head, she says, "What you need?"

"Coffee," I say.

She doesn't get up. She has a full face of make-up and is still wearing her terrycloth robe. Her red hair is in curlers. She starts humming. We are always in some state of crossing a room, incongruent parts of the same machine. This is marriage.

The second time I saw Penny she gave me a book. It was *The Beast in The Jungle*, which I hadn't read in years. She has a way of thrusting a gift, or a glass of something into your hands as if she wants to dispose of it. It's how she deals with exposure. I used to be the same way. I never stayed in bed after sex. I'd take my exit on the way to the bathroom. I didn't understand that remaining there next to a woman you'd just slept with wasn't a promise. It was just a nap. I'd often wake up in her tiny studio to the smell of pancakes. She likes breakfast for lunch. Sometimes I'd open my eyes to see hers aimed right at me. The whole idea of watching people sleep befuddled me. Why intrude on the one time you don't have to worry about what people think of you? She wrote something on the title page of the book, but I couldn't make much of it. I slid the novella into the stacks that surround my desk. My bookshelves had long since overflowed. I worried that Beth might notice it. A fool's thought. As if this slim volume would blare like a pair of red panties.

The day before Thanksgiving I went out to get a cup of coffee. I avoided Penny's neighborhood even though they make better espresso there. It took some restraint to not make a left at Talmadge, knock on the door of her studio, wait until she answered in her oversized T-shirt, obviously a hand-me-down — I dared not guess from whom. The *You Are Here* printed on it mocking and sardonic. Sometimes I'd put my hand up her shirt and that would be that. It was better to picture the door slammed in my face the last time I was there, it helped I had never heard her utter the word *sorry*. She wanted me gone? Fine. I was gone.

I chose a coffee shop at a busy intersection. I sat outside to read the paper. I was procrastinating on the Austen thing, and missing a girl. It had been years since I'd done that. I felt foolish, and, frankly, pissed. Certainly she wasn't pacing the floor about me,

MARK A. RODRIGUEZ, *CUPIE*, 2015. PHOTO: JEFF MCLANE

although I hoped. Sidewalk cafes in this neighborhood always meant a lot of exhaust. There was a woman about 40 in an SUV stopped at the light. She was weeping into her hands. In that moment I hoped the worst for Penny, and regretted having given her anything.

Outside my study window the trees are doing what they are supposed to, dropping their yellows and auburns. Southern California does its best impression of fall. The rattling has calmed in the kitchen; Beth is now in our bedroom pulling up her black stockings. I know this because I can hear that jump she makes as she jerks them over her dimpled thighs.

Sam had come in late the night before; now he scuffles into the kitchen. The girl is right behind him. A tangle of her blond hair makes its way north, but roots of her hair sprout a candid dark brown. She is wearing what are most likely his pajamas. They both notice me by the coffee pot waiting for the first cup. The counters are covered with pies, casseroles and serving dishes. It looks like the preparations for a funeral reception.

He scans the kitchen. "And so it begins."

"Yes, your mom went a little nuts this year. Great to see you, bud."

I embrace him; he feels thicker. I stare at the girl, who now crosses her arms over her chest. I guess she is braless.

"Oh, Pop: This is Aimee."

She reaches out, still with one hand across her chest. She is tall, as promised.

"It's with an I and an E."

"Good to know," I say.

I remember Beth at 22, in jean shorts, and a smile that felt like you won something. She and I went to the same Laundromat near USC. She always wanted to know what I was reading, and what I thought of it. I'd watch her lift her whites into the dryer. She was working at a nonprofit; she called herself an activist, but I wanted her anyway. Beth was on every committee to stop one thing or another. She often talked away with her head in the dryer, so she never knew how I stared at her legs. It seemed then that we would never run out of things to say.

We are all cleaned up and seated now. Aimee is wearing a thin, yellow sweater with holes in it, and she immediately starts in on the chardonnay. Sam wears a tie and has his hair slicked back. He really is a business major, but the tie seems to be mocking the whole occasion. I try to hide my nervousness by cleaning my glasses with the edge of the tablecloth. He has his mother's blue eyes, but he got my mouth. Many people have told me they think I'm unapproachable because my face rests in a frown. I hide mine with a beard. My father bore the same look, and on the occasion when he would smile he was momentarily unrecognizable. Sam has just the right amount of dryness to pull off the turned down corners of his lips.

Beth is in a tight black dress. "I think the turkey died twice," she says, "once on the farm, and once in my kitchen. Sorry, Aimee." I added another word to my list: guileless. She's been pointing remarks at Aimee all morning trying to make the girl feel at home.

Aimee squirms as if she's been called to attention. Sam answers for her, "Mom, *you* didn't cook it."

"Honey," she says, "it's the one thing I did cook."

The long stem candles are lit. The napkins fanned. She is fussing over rolls and refusing help. She has not stopped moving since we took our places. Penny has yet to arrive. Her chair is next to Beth's and across from mine, just as it was a year ago. It's too early for me to be relieved. I start in on the chardonnay too. I remember her punctuality is always poor.

Beth appears from the kitchen again. "So Aimee, what are you studying?" Aimee turns to Sam.

"I was studying fashion design. But, I'm taking a second."

Sam shakes his head. "She dropped out," he says. "So did I. Can we not make a production out of it?"

Beth is staring across the room at me, wearing an oven mitt. I notice her apron: two embroidered hens face to face saying, "Pluck you!" This is a parenting moment. Her eyes tell me: You'd better say the right thing here.

I lift up my glass at him and say, "To the adventure."

Beth says, "We'll talk about this later."

She could've guessed I would side with the kid. Aimee clinks my glass, and for the first time since entering our house she appears relaxed. My son killed a boy. You live alone with that. Any of his other mistakes seem trivial in comparison.

Now Beth will be pissed at me for sure.

Penny's chair is still empty. Beth disappears into the kitchen again. The food is getting cold. I'm just sitting there waiting to be served. With Aimee draped on Sam he couldn't care less about his father. I could prod her about her plans, but it seems like a lost cause. She'll pass, and in a semester he'll meet a new girl.

Beth comes from the kitchen with the turkey, "I think we should go on without Penelope," she says. "It's odd she hasn't called."

"Yes, let's eat," I say.

We start filling our plates.

"Is she still trying to be a painter?" Sam says.

"Who's Penelope?" Aimee says.

"She's my goddaughter." Beth sets the bird down unsteadily. It's skeletal and overcooked — more buzzard than turkey.

I stuff a dinner roll in my mouth so I don't have to respond to Sam.

Beth slips off her oven mitts and says, "I think she's still painting. Although I haven't talked to her much lately."

When the doorbell rings my face is in my wine glass. I try to not act startled. Beth is in the kitchen searching for the carving knives. It rings again.

The wind is cutting through the maples, and when I open the door it's lifted her hair and obscured her face. I feel horrible that it's so good to see her. She's put in an effort for the occasion. She hooks the wild strand behind her ear. Her hair is down and straight, the black of it framing her face just right. Her lips are red. She's wearing a pleated skirt (I've never seen her in a skirt). I hope this is for my benefit.

She says, "I can't stay long," and pushes past me as if I'm a bouncer.

There they are, sitting side by side, my wife and, I guess, my ex-lover. I know how they both cross a room naked, how Beth hides her stomach. Her legs were once fine and lean — after Sam, turned thick and sturdy. Penny didn't care much about nudity — it was a slipshod weapon. She spent most afternoons at home undressed with her robe open, her petite body followed by a wave of silk when she ran to turn the kettle off. Her small perky breasts ready for lips and hands. In profile they sometimes reminded me of puppies with brown noses.

Watching her now with a knife in her hand cutting through the tough bird that Beth cooked is — as Penny once said herself — "much sadder" than I expected.

She looks around for a moment before she lifts her glass, as if she's seeing our dining room for the first time. The large, gold-framed mirror that'd been passed down to Beth from a grandparent. We'd moved that thing in every apartment we owned, sometimes we leaned it on the floor because our walls were not big enough, or grand enough to hold it. For a second I thought of all the things it had reflected. Once I caught Sam as a toddler kissing his own image, his tiny hands fogging and trying to grip the glass. I stopped the thing from toppling on him. Beth and I had made love in front it, in our first and incredibly tiny apartment in college. A mattress on the hardwood floor, the gold mirror in front of it, she said it was very Parisian; I just liked watching her milky ass rise in the air. I moved it the next week once I discovered that I didn't much like seeing myself reading, jacking off, or eating ice cream. I wanted to change the channel.

The silk white curtains, the glass and bullion chandelier, the mahogany table — all of that was new, a bit gauche, and it seemed to outdo us. Beth liked things that had history, or appeared to anyway. I was only a few years older than her, but she joked that I, too, was vintage. The only thing the gold mirror reflects now are the tops of our bobbing foreheads (my thinning hair), and the crystal, glass drops of the chandelier. Penny studies it, maybe as a relic of a marriage, maybe checking the exits, or perhaps she was noticing how little of me was in this room. She then scans the guests at the table. Everyone is slicing, pouring gravy, buttering rolls, except me. I am lost in an occupation that is only employed by her presence — willful admiration. She observes the entire room without once stopping on my face.

J. M. W. Turner was afraid of anyone apprehending his process, so his father was his only assistant. He felt the other painters of his time were all gaining on him. I never asked Penny why she loved Turner so much, but it seemed a logical first crush. While ladling on the green beans, I see Sam staring at Penny. Usually when in the same room, they act like benign cousins. Watching him makes me even less hungry. I set my fork down. He will never be handsome, although he will be bright. He told Beth last week that he feels himself getting older (she laughed) and that he's sure now he doesn't want kids. I don't know if Sam would trust me as Turner trusted his father. I don't think I own a single secret of his. Beth was the one to wipe his wet eyes, or press a Kleenex to his face and say, *blow*.

The two young women at the table are divergent creatures. Aimee with her bobbed, blond hair and dark roots, distracted eyes — clinging to Sam like a last cigarette. You can tell that she has not seen real disappointment. Maybe that's why Sam is fond of her. She is timid, but even more so, she wishes to be left to her tiny wants and desires. When she seeks my son's arm, she leans in to find his attention again. Her concerns can be read across a room; Penny's never can. Although she is young, Penny makes every effort to never be the last to know. She is frightened to be seen as unintelligent, or worse, uninteresting. Yes, she is, I guess, prettier than Aimee, but her countenance is just more refined, and it seemed in this moment that Sam also notices the difference. He holds the expression of a young man on the verge of a question, a face I had seen a hundred times in my classroom.

As I reach for the bottle of chardonnay, Aimee rests her hand on Sam's back. It is only then that he breaks his gaze from Penny and takes another roll. I exhale. Clearly Aimee is not utterly dense, she has bet on a horse in this room too. Aimee checks Penny out in between sips. When Penny looks in her direction, it is severe and sharp. Like she is side-glancing a fellow sprinter before they begin the 50-meter. For a moment I feel a tinge of empathy for Aimee with an I and an E.

When they were introduced, Penny did not close her hand around Aimee's. She kept it open like a mannequin's. The handshake was not one at all — it was an inspection. Penny had always been the only young woman at our table. Beth embraced Penny longer than usual, much like she hugs Sam when he comes home. When she went to sit down at the table I saw in Penny's normally poised nature a flutter of unsteadiness.

"That is such a sweet sweater Aimee. Did you make it yourself?" Penny says.

Sam looks at her sweater beside him, as if he is seeing it anew. Aimee says, "I got it at Barneys."

Penny says, "Cool."

Sam's eyes find Penny's again.

This is not a word she would use. *Cool.* I am the only one to pick up how foreign it sounds.

In that instant Penny wipes her mouth, makes eye contact with me for the first time, and shrugs. A white flag? I want to grab her then by her slender shoulders. The way I would after a fight, or a week of miscommunication. I wanted to own that mouth. I wanted to crease her thoughts with me forever. The truth was, she'd always be that slippery ache, impossible to dispose of. This would probably haunt me much longer than it would her. I was a momentarily improvident choice, a bit role in the long life of a beautiful girl. I would no longer see her in that studio doorway half-dressed in a T-shirt, panties, and paint.

It was in this moment that it added up. The connection I failed to make, that so plainly was before me now. *You Are Here.* That T-shirt she'd worn around the house. I'd bought the damned thing for Sam — I mean, Beth had bought it as a Christmas present, and in high school he'd worn it until it stank. It was soft, and once black, now worn to gray. On the front of it, the Milky Way, with an arrow pointing to Earth — to those words. After Sam went to college it disappeared until it was on the frame of this woman, this distraction. When the constellation was right in front of me I'd just reach under it, only caring for it to be removed.

I excuse myself. Beth is busy asking Aimee questions about fashion. I do not raise my eyes to see Penny's face. It is my lone chair that groans as I get up and go upstairs to my study. I take two steps at a time. Of course. They're around the same age; when he'd come home from college he'd leave for nights on end. I scan the spines of books on the shelves, then the stacks on the floor, and there it is: the slim little gift I had hidden so well from myself shoved near the bottom.

I open the flap to her inscription: "The moon is up, and yet it is not night, / The sun as yet divides the day with her." The Byron poem. This line was on the museum label next to the Turner painting. She had already seen it. Penny had been there before. Those tears were not for *Modern Rome — Campo Vaccino.*

I hear footsteps coming up the stairs, and I look up. Beth is still wearing her apron. "Honey," she says, "what are you *doing*?"

POEM BEFORE A VERDICT

CATHY LINH CHE

Once, in Long Beach,
when my mother said
No English,

the solicitor told her
to go back to the jungle
where she came from.

She taught me
the names of flowers.
Years later

I learned
their names
in English –

narcissus,
rhododendron,
chrysanthemum.

The words placed me
firmly
in this country,

though I slipped
from one language
to the other –

amphibian.

Once, as a child,
I coughed and ear-ached
and cried in a new home.

Tora! Tora! Tora! thundered
on the television. Warplanes
dropped bombs like so much

weight. My parents slept
in that blue light. Their
eyelids shuddered.

I imagined
that light to be
another country.

What do the men see
when the say, *Ni hao*
and Konichiwa?

A police officer
once aimed his eye up
the length of my leg

as I descended
the subway stairs.
What could I do then?

When I was a girl,
my mother was arrested
and placed in a cell.

The officer did not cuff her
in front of us
because we surrounded her

like small animals
reciting the tricks
we learned at school.

Soldiers called
my grandmother
mama-san.

She was a lucky one:
just one lost daughter,
and grandchildren

who grew limbs
in another country –
where they spoke

the language
of soldiers.
Their eyes shone

with the milk
their motherland
could not afford.

Today, I am singing

their old songs: chorus
of my mother's heartbreaks,

my father a soldier
in a long-ago war,
my brother's voice

ricocheting
through the phone line
on October 10,

when he was held at gun point
in Liberty Park.
Don't tell mom,

he says. He wears
a black bracelet,
etched 10/10 to remember.

Soldiers touched my mother's hair.
My great-grandfather was cut down
by an American plane.

My mother says, *In Vietnam,*
a life means so little.
What does a life mean, then,

in America? If smoke is a prayer,
I trace its dark rise.
If prayers are a way into memory,

let me construct a burning image.
Let my voice go hoarse.
Let me light these damn words on fire.

FORGIVENESS

CATHY LINH CHE

Last night, I dreamt my cousin
was next to me, his zipper open,
his sex rubbed raw. He razored

the calluses from his feet,
sometimes so close to the flesh
that he drew blood.

That skin a pile, gathering.
When I was 11, he tickled me
until I gasped, until breath

became a prayer only
intermittently answered.
No, I said. *Stop!*

He didn't stop until
I threw up.
Do you love me? he asked.

Yes, I said. *Because you*
are my cousin. I unzipped
the wall and stepped

all the way in. Once he slid down
my pants and slipped in
his tongue. When I wept,

he said, *Không phá chim nũa*,
and pulled up my pants.
I punched his arms as he laughed.

I ran, but he planted a house
two blocks from my own.
He sired a child, a boy

with smooth, white skin.
I look in the mirror and see my face.
I close my eyes and see his ghost.

His body across the tracks.
My body solid in a chair
in a coffee shop in Minneapolis.

In the parking lot, my friends sit
waiting for me, and I zip my body up
in order to meet them.

CASEMENTS

CARMIEL BANASKY

BECAUSE OF YOUR name, and mine. Because we were seated in the A's in class, until your mother changed your name back to W when she found out what your father did. Because of your shoulders. Because you flicked those wet blue rubber bands from your braces at me, and I scooted my chair in closer anyway so you could you cheat off my spelling test. Because, in the girls' bathroom, I let you dig your hand down my pants, and you were angry with me for standing still like a chump while you showed me what boys wanted. Because your lessons didn't work, because the boys teemed to you like jellyfish, and you lied to me and said they liked me, too, because you didn't care my chest was flat and that I hid behind the taxi row on First Street. Because you didn't eat much, due to the braces, you said. Because, in the subway, you gave me a bloody nose to show me how it's done.

Because I was scared of you after you told me what your father did. Because what did I know. Because I went to California and you went to college. Because you dropped out after your first year and I found you on my broken porch, swollen with rain. Because you said it wouldn't be the last time you'd show up like a stray dog.

Because your mother lost her head. Because you went home to find it. Because we drove back east in a rickety hearse we would deliver to a funeral home. Because we couldn't afford another way, and I wouldn't let you go alone. Because it smelled of daffodils and bleach. Because, by the time you reached her, your mother had forgotten your name. So, because of illness, but not because of that at all. Because of Clinton Street, where your mother died while I was scoring us weed. Because of cottage cheese and fruit, and the year you ate nothing else, because of your mother, you said, and you looked like a knobby strand of kelp.

Because we lay on Rockaway Beach as if we were alone, and I touched your see-through spine and said you were so thin I could break you. Because you pushed my hand away, because you left me at low tide, because I told you you were sick.

Because the next I heard from you, was with an invitation. Because I watched you marry under rose blossoms siphoned from another season, and you seemed healthy in New England fog, and it had nothing to do with me. Because you changed your name to his, which happened to be back to A. Because the man was not a bad man, if a little nasally, and I could tell you meant to love him. Because, after the toasts, after the oysters, and the first dance meant for your missing dad, I saw the way you shrunk when you thought no one was watching.

Because of your boilerplate Christmas cards, but more because of a Polaroid I kept, tucked in the frame of a picture of newer people, where you're sprawled over a speed bump in some unremarkable parking lot. Because we didn't speak for 28 years. Because of how easily we recognized each other on the same stalled subway car, two old women in a snowstorm that bit out the lights. Because the shadows were prehistoric, and in the darkness we held each other, and I cried because your silver hair slid into my eyes. Because we let go again when the train began to move. Because he never wanted children, you said. Because I didn't tell you then that I'd raised two kids on my own and they saw me through law school. Because the next year saw you sick, this time like your mother, and the husband was good but not good enough, and because you showed up on my stoop in Fort Greene, again in the rain, with an umbrella you closed much too soon, because, you said, you didn't want him taking care of you.

Because it was the hand your mother dealt you, and you said she didn't mean it, and wasn't it funny. Because you stared at my children's photos on the wall as if they were yours. Because of the teacups you threw at my head and the names you called me that I won't repeat. Because that wasn't you; because it was. Because we sat by the window each morning, watching the wind move, and on your good days you made fun of me and claimed I had more wrinkles than you, you'd counted every one. Because we slow-danced as I half-carried you from the chair to the bed. Because, this time, I did not tell you to eat. Because I trusted you knew what to do. Because you never pretended with me, and I watched your parched smile flake away like fish scales. Because your eyes went gray. Because you ceased to know me.

But I knew you. Because I knew you before forgetting, before we knew what it was to dance or kiss or fall off a bike, and before we knew the word for Alzheimer's, before one hundred species of trees, and by two oceans and across a continent, and across years of not knowing, before we knew we knew anything, and then when you knew nothing again. Always, we are 13, sprawled on the grass median, up to no good.

❖

VLADIMIR DE JESUS SANTOS, INK ON PAPER, 2013.

THE FUTURE MAYOR OF LOS ANGELES IS CURRENTLY ON ADDERALL

MICHAEL LORENZO PORTER

"Anyone who ever thought too much of money could never have enough."

Los Angeles.

Ever heard of it?

There's lots of murder here.

I said a fuck ton of murder.

There are other things too, like heart attacks and cats, but mostly murder. This town runs on it (murder).

Sometimes, even the LAPD gets to murder people. It's an undeniable fact that Los Angeles absolutely loves its murderers. Luckily they have a great variety to choose from.

I guess I'm a coward most nights. A flat-out Adderall abuser to my awful core.

I'm a catty teenage girl with no soul. I'm Barry Bonds.

I'm poison.

I'm listening to the radio police-scanner app on my new phone. My hands sweat as the calls come through. "Potential B and E in Westwood." "Carjacking in progress at the corner of Hollywood and Western." "Group of black teens playing in the park."

The juiciest frequency is, of course, the Highway Patrol frequency. All the action takes place there. I can sense that these late-night Adderall binges spent getting cozy with the vernacular of our local boys in blue have helped paint a pretty clear picture for me. I'm already over-qualified to be the mayor of this fine city.

For now, I have fashioned some kind of living out of writing and teaching middle-schoolers how to project their tiny voices while on stage. This is called performing arts. The kids are full of energy. Energy they don't know what to do with. I want to inspire them. Speeches, I seem to recall, have been known to inspire not-so-great men to do extraordinary things. I won't list any examples. You should use the first one that came to mind. My speech will follow a short clip of Russell Crowe's speech after winning his Oscar for *Gladiator* and will sound something like this:

"Now. How many of you have Instagram?" I expect most hands will rise. "Dabble with video do you? Try this: Mute your cartoons or clips of cartoons you now call cartoons and play a song. Change the feeling you feel as Daffy Duck takes shotgun shells to the solar plexus. To the ribs, and then to the face. Click play on your douchebag stepdad's iPod and if Daniel Powter's 'Bad Day' starts playing, congratulations, you've suddenly created a pitch-perfect comedy centered around our obsession with violence, not just as singular people, but as a nation and as a global race, and why for the past three decades (if not longer), we have not addressed how desensitization more than daddy and mommy not being home and even more than *Halo* or *Call of Duty* or *Grand Theft Auto* is responsible for the foul-mouthed army of Neo-Nazis dedicated solely to exercising their tongues and thumbs via Xbox Live by doling out no less than 87 uses of the word nigger per hour."

But maybe that will be too much for them. Maybe I will just keep preaching the importance of feeling important in a world so intently focused on making you feel that you are not. I could also explain that it only matters that you feel important, not that you actually are important because let's face it — not all of you are important. But that doesn't mean you don't have the right to feel important.

Maybe they will get it. Maybe they are smarter than me. I inhale another 30mg.

Back at home. On the tube, an ad for a fictional policeman show flashes across the set.

A hero cop becomes a national hero after saving a child from what appears to be a run-of-the-mill burning building rescue, only to be revealed much later that it had been a drug deal gone awry. They use Bowie for the background music and I'm sick for him. And what's more, the whole plot, arc, and story have been told in 30 seconds.

I'm late for work.

NPR is on really loud in the Prius. Osmosis?

Jay seems alert and especially in tune with the wave of traffic in front of us. On the radio, there is talk of radioactive wolves not only living but thriving near the location of the Chernobyl Incident, 30 years later. The area is of note due to it being notorious for its potential to be radioactive for at least the next 350,000 years. I rack my brain for a solution as I chase an Addy with warm ginger beer that was left unsupervised in the backseat all weekend.

Come to Daddy.

If anyone knows anything about wolves, it's Master Miller. I tap my codec and let him know everything pertaining to the radioactive wolves as I currently understand it.

He understands. A call will be made to Pliskin.

I turn off my codec and it dawns on me that I forgot to tell him happy birthday, but it's okay because he never remembers mine anyway.

We are almost in Arcadia now. Almost time to turn on the lights and attempt something resembling a fully functioning adult human man. I make out "Persuasive Essay" in bold letters in pink dry erase marker on the board, and then when pink runs out, green. The children groan in sync. They share a decidedly acute disdain for writing assignments of virtually any kind, and this piece of truth crushes me infinitely.

"Guys, don't think of it as an essay per se." A much softer set of groans can be heard, but they are of the curious variety and aren't as unified as the previous set. I continue. "Listen up. I'm the judge. You're the lawyer. Persuade me that your client is not guilty of the crimes for which they have been charged." *Oohs* and *ahhs* decorate the sound waves.

I particularly enjoy little Jane's essay on why the Joker should not be held accountable for his murder of the vigilante known as Batman because she truly believes that Batman and the Joker stand for something bigger than just themselves. In her very subtle style, she explains to me that Batman only exists as a very ugly representation of America's current state of affairs when concerning politics and the treatment of its people, while the Joker is in many ways a product of a radically expansive and diverse terrorist network, which exists as an answer to the long-standing, and rarely addressed heavy-handed police responses to critical issues facing poor people in this country.

Grab the gun. Plant the gun. Shoot the gun. Buy the gun. Love the gun. Be sure to make it your friend. Be the gun. Love guns more than your friends, your kids and yourself. Die by the gun. Police brutality. Torture. Unlawful government surveillance of its citizens. Etc.

I awarded the paper, an A+. Not because she earned it, though she did, but because I have always dreamt of having a piece of paper with my name on it hanging on a fridge with an A+ in the top right corner. I sign all A+ papers with my three initials as if to certify this rare feat. This perfect game of the educational world. Take a bow, young flamethrower.

You're a winner.

My last visit to Palm Springs was actually the first and well, coincidentally, the very last. I bumped into several species of dinosaur that I, a man of decent common sense and a genuinely healthy mind of no more than 30 years and eight months of age, wholeheartedly believed to be extinct for at least the better half of the previous 10,000 years.

I was wrong.

There they were — right in front of me! There was the T-Rex buying two tall PBRs at the 76 station while Joy slept silently in the Prius. Six o'clock. There's another lizard person with tough, rock skin that's more orange than Dallas Raines with the contrast on your TV set boosted to the max. Her lizard eyes pick up my gaze and she slips into a shadow. Gone.

Seven o'clock. Denny's.

A kind of pterodactyl man wearing an entire suit of denim, could be seen putting on a brilliant little one-man show for whoever has the time to listen. Whoever has time to spend burning up in the 105 degree sun that we oh so fucking deserve. Time to watch a madman burn.

"You, me, we're all gonna die! No one lives in the future. This ends here! They aren't coming back!"

He runs off. He's heading for the street, and is nearly obliterated by a bright yellow Dodge Ram pickup. Swiped him at least. He's down, but not out.

I watch him for a little. I see him pick himself up.

I'm back in the Prius. I lean my chair way back and nap. Maybe when I open my eyes, the wind won't be so punishing. The drive from Arizona has been long.

When I wake up, Jay's face is covered with a thin layer of sweat and I laugh at her.

I'm a monster.

I'm passing out.

Later.

Right up against my fucking window!

A velociraptor with a Slurpee cup. He jangles the cup. I look away. Not in horror, but in confusion. These dragon-skinned people were never meant to inhabit this habitat long-term. They are invaders. I take out the pocket Purple Majesty notebook and write a note to myself:

"Find out who the mayor of Palm Springs is. Find out if Palm Springs will be in my jurisdiction once I become mayor of Los Angeles."

On a different day entirely, I'm grappling with a beast at Guido's on Santa Monica. I am mentally preparing my exit strategy for a lunch meeting with Jack Hanna.

Yes. That Jack Hanna.

He got drunk, which is neither shocking nor important. He gets drunk every time we meet. He claims to know the Garcetti family. "Tight like a fucking drum" he says. He slaps the table like a drum and bites his bottom lip. Buffoon.

I wonder out loud how long it will take to setup a meeting with the Garcettis and how quickly they can endorse me for mayor once I've shown them my proposals — one of which is something I can only refer to as the Spider Extermination Commission, or SEXC.

He pretends not to hear. I lean in.

"When the fuck can I meet them?"

"You'll meet them when you meet them."

A stray piece of rigatoni falls out of his mouth. An elderly woman notices it, and I've never been this low.

Jack says he believes in me and my policies even though he has not one goddamn idea what they might be.

None.

Do I know?

Jack Hanna calls the waiter over.

"Two more whiskeys."

Maybe I'll stay.

Jack Hanna knows me. I know him. Jack Hanna is my friend.

Much later.

Let's see if I have time to make a federal case against the great state of California centered around ethnic insensitivity. A case about you, me, and who the fuck we should look to. Who in fuck we should look up to at this point in time. At this point in time, a great many of you believe in your heart that you are heading toward a destiny or fate in which you will be rewarded for doing what in any real society — any real advanced, educated, and human society — would be considered the bare minimum.

I was asked to leave the Starbucks. Removed from my soapbox.

I was removed from the Starbucks.

"I'll take my business *elsewhere*!"

The police are here. I don't talk to cops, though.

I head for Winchell's on Venice.

I rifle through the pockets of my gray tweed jacket.

Jackpot. 30 mg of joy. No chaser. Smooth.

Valley Village, Inglewood, NoHo, Koreatown, Frog Town, Downtown, Hollywood, Watts, and Culver City.

Thursday is apartment hunting day. Our lease is almost up at The Harvard. The search has become frantic, yet focused. $1,100. One bed (or studio). Pets allowed. Central air. And so on and on and on and on and on.

I am enjoying my early morning evacuation of an undercooked Philly cheesesteak. There's '70s glam rock on the AM/FM radio in the bathroom. I hear a couple fighting in the alley. A gate slams. A woman screams. I shut the window. There's a knock at the door. It's Jay. She's holding a small baggie and a glass marijuana pipe with some cruddy orange paint on it. "I farted. It's gonna smell a little," I joke.

She puts the pipe and bag down on the sink. I wipe, then flush and proceed to pack the bowl without washing my hands. Jay puffs the pipe while fixing a hazel eye on the alley below. There's someone down there. An elderly man with a cartoonish curvature of his spine and what appears to be his son are ambling toward an already running, late-'80s Cadillac. The car is exceptionally clean. It literally purrs while black smoke puffs out like tobacco from a champion's freshly lit cigar.

The spoils of victory. The boy does not assist the man in his quest to sit in the driver's seat so that he may pilot his black chariot of infirmity. He watches as a machine, a motorized walker, does its best to propel the old man into a position of power — or at least one of mobility and dignity. Jay looks toward the hilltop overlooking the alley.

"That's the Black Beverly Hills." Jay, very softly: "There are people up there."

I take a puff as if to numb myself in regards to what I am witnessing outside the window — through the screen, and most importantly, right in front of me. "Those people — the ones living atop the hill, they could see us if they maybe had a telescope," I snap. Her gaze won't shift. "All they would see is you video recording that old man getting into his car. Then who would be wasting their time?" I ponder her query, but only internally.

Unsure of how much time has passed, I respond: "I'm starting to think they will never see us. Telescope or not. We are not planets in a distant galaxy with the gravitational pull of all your worst nightmares come to life. We are not conjured up out of all this death. We live here too. Down below. Don't you get it? It's *Rear Window* through a classist lens that's laughably out of focus when it comes to issues of the haves and have-nots. The rich watch the poor while the poor observe the elderly become dependent upon technologies they do not understand."

My phone rings.

It's Jack Hanna.

Jay smiles at me. I pop another 30mg and chase it with sink water.

My head hurts.

Jack Hanna is on speaker asking me about what my policies are. I tell him I'll call him later and he seems genuinely disappointed. I smile into the mirror.

Sat down too fast in a downtown bar last Saturday night and became dizzy. Dizziness always makes me think of death. The thought vanished almost as quickly as the next round of poison arrived. We were having a few. Just the guys. The bar was cold. The beer was lukewarm. It was July outside and Hoth inside. An A/C unit had caused some kind of an outage, shorting the fridge — and now, like the energy parasite it was, it continued on living and keeping us cool while our beers died a thousand deaths before finding relief in the afterlife. In our chilled bellies.

Everyone in the bar was alone.

I wake up in the bathroom, again. Now I'm alone. The house is quiet. Alone is the best-case scenario for so many out of whack Angelenos. Death is truthfully the real and optimal best-case scenario, but for the sake of this exercise in fictional scenarios, let's pretend that it's "alone." Now try and pretend that you are not (alone). Join the circus.

Start a cult, and let me fucking join it! Do it wrong, get the fall guy in trouble (you'll know him when you see him). Lie in open court, just like your mother and father taught you. Pursue that almighty dollar with everything you have to give, and when you've given all you can, steal it from the next man and make him give all he can until he's just skin being dragged behind you in a cart that you're too embarrassed to just "leave somewhere" despite the flies and the rot and the shit that's still stuck inside him. Despite every single lie you learned in school. This is how the world works. Take. Take Take Take Take Take Take Take Take Take the red pill, my hand and this copy of *The Illuminati for Dummies*.

Fucking Jack Hanna is calling me. I turn away from the mirror to take the call.

He's screaming.

I pull the phone away from my ear and end the call.

NPR is on at a pretty acceptable volume. The featured guest is a journalist claiming to have heard wolves howling near the wreckage of Chernobyl which happened about 30 years ago. I want to write about this because surely, now they're "super wolves", but I'd much rather speak with them in the hopes of gaining some insight as to how they are surviving considering the severity of their conditions. I would ask how they feel about the fact that rabbits don't live long enough to get cancer, so they remain largely unaffected by the disaster. I would ask them if they feel powerful when killing something at a disadvantage in every measurable category. I'd ask them what it feels like to be alive, and what time means to them.

Oh, what a time to be alive.

Later that night, in a different part of town called Downtown, a man and his confusion go salsa dancing together on the metro red line.

Oh, it's definitely the eyes that get me the most. So many pairs of beautiful eyes. Light eyes. Dark eyes. Mysterious and dusty, soot-filled eyes redder than Mars and hotter than a Sun that melts my chocolate chip cookie dough ice cream get rich quick scheme.

How long is this train ride?

I take note of my surroundings in accordance with my most valued and treasured survival tactics. No threat assessed. Everything is calm except for the train as it moves along at what must be hyper-speed that's been sped up by drugs and innate paranoia. I'm not blinking anymore.

Jay and I arrive in Hollywood, completely weightless, and I am ready to talk, but the best I can grasp at from the carousel of thoughts sounds like this: "I had that dream again." Feigned intrigue on her face.

"I'm Luke, and you're Loretta", I snarl through a catlike grin as if this phrase could hold some heartfelt meaning to her. I keep smiling through her confusion. She kisses me goodbye, and walks up the stairs to her apartment. No one looks back. Anyway, I have to go. I'm late for lunch with Jack Hanna. He promised we'd go over my first proposal today. He says we can discuss the Spider Extermination Commission.

I'm a man about town. People think the best of me. I am in control.

At the restaurant, Jack is wearing shorts again even though I explicitly told him not to do so in my presence. He is also blindingly drunk. I'm starting to think Jack is using me for my restaurant connections. I sit across from him with what I hope he understands is more than just slight contempt and place several empty wine bottles on the floor at his feet.

Jack is already eating his favorite dish — seafood pasta with red sauce. Jack is the type of person who isn't too famous to hand out business cards.

I'm pretty sure Jack Hanna has cryptomnesia.

He keeps giving me these hideous business cards of his, and we've been acquainted for the better of six months. Late last night, I used one of his business cards to pick up a piece of Ani's dog shit, and I've never felt more alive.

The waiter walks over, but I don't get to order because Jack insists that we need more time even though he's already eating.

I should let his wife know that he's up to his old tricks — that he's been smoking those ungodly Marlboro Golds again. Jack Hanna is a trainwreck.

I can't sabotage his marriage. Not yet anyway. Although, it would bring me (I imagine) an unsafe level of elation and/or giddiness. It's not that I'm interested in Jack Hanna's wife. I'm not. But I am very much invested in Jack Hanna's unhappiness. All of that has to wait, though. He keeps hanging the fucking Garcettis over me like a carrot in front of some distinguished Philly down at Hollywood Park.

I know they are my in.

This is how I take the city back from the crooks — from the inept $3,000-three-piece-suit-wearing, buy-one-get-one-free, does-anybody-have-change-for-a-nickel, dime-a-dozen, self-aggrandizing politicians who currently hold this vice-like grip on my sweet City of the Angels.

This is how I interrupt the uptight clown show.

Jack Hanna is blacked out at the table.

I am Jack's hatred of self — manifested as an entirely real person who participates in actual events, and can prove with some quickness I might add, that he is real — if such proof is ever deemed necessary in a court of law or any entity operating as a court of public opinion wherein said public opinion could result in public execution or stoning.

Later on, I feel alone enough to prepare a speech in the event that I do actually win the election this fall. I decide to wing it, and I begin to take shots at myself in the mirror.

I'm Clint Eastwood.

I can't miss.

Headshot.

Deadpool.

I'm still breathing.

I imagine someone in the imaginary crowd asks me about my beliefs, my principles, ideals, or any combination of those words or their synonyms.

"Ladies and gentlemen … I've traveled over half our state to be here tonight. I just couldn't get away sooner. Yes. What is it exactly that I believe? That's the question, isn't it? What are the things that I hold closest in the hour of deepest despair? The trying times of self-doubt and ugliness. I think you will find this refreshing. No, not a bottomless glass of lemonade in hell refreshing, but refreshing all the same. I can start by saying that in stark contrast to my own somewhat sarcastic, yet most cherished upheld ideals about what a man should seek to accomplish versus what man is (based upon thousands of years of human history) more realistically, almost tragically destined to accomplish, are the beliefs of a man I have come to know over the course of a very tumultuous, bewildering, and rewarding 30 years of friendship.

I would like to announce my running mate!"

"Leachim Oznerol Retrop!"

It's Tuesday again, and I'm just getting to the campaign headquarters. Things are picking up nicely.

My smile fades just as I crack open the door.

Jack Hanna is asleep on the floor. Poor bastard.

It's my own doing, though. I told him he could sleep here, unsupervised, so long as he agreed to sleep on the floor.

Judging by the hitch in his step, he took my directions seriously as he seems to have suffered some sort of hip damage. I smile a wicked smile, internally.

Of course, he's only here because Jackie Hanna threw him out after finding a very carefully placed pack of Gold's in Jack's camera bag. I know I said I'd wait, but I've been acting on compulsions more and more, and the results have been astounding. I am brilliant. I am a genius. I am the voice of a generation of sheep. I toss a fucking Adderall down the gullet because I have an inexhaustible supply.

I think about calling into work dead.

The phone rings — interrupting *The Bill Simmons Podcast*. An unknown number appears at the top of the screen.

The voice says that he is Gil Garcetti.

"I'm Donald Duck."

Gil doesn't laugh, but instead asks if this is a "bad time."

I run the hurry up.

"I'm busy," I retort.

The word "lunch" makes an appearance. It's quickly followed by the voice inside and outside my head: "I'm listening."

A lunch is scheduled.

A sleepy Jack Hanna winks at me from the wet bar.

I glare at him and deduce the meaning of the look in his eyes to be that he is afraid of me.

I am in complete control.

VLADIMIR DE JESUS SANTOS, INK ON PAPER.

GIG ECONOMY

DANIEL OLIVAS

THE YOUNG LAWYER stands on the sidewalk outside the Ronald Reagan State Building on Spring Street. He hums, swings his briefcase from side to side, pleased with himself, waiting for his Uber to arrive and whisk him off to the Burbank Airport. The Los Angeles afternoon sun makes his already damp dress shirt adhere to the soft contours of his torso. He's gained another 10 pounds in the last two months; the late nights at the large, San Francisco firm combined with takeout Chinese, Thai, and Mexican food all taking a toll on his once lean body. But he is successful, getting top performance reviews from the partners, veiled promises of great things to come in his career. Few young associates would get the opportunity to argue an appellate case as he just did, on an important contract dispute that could make great authority if the court sides with him and issues a favorable, published opinion. Creating *stare decisis*, a decision that will be cited by the legal treatises, taught in law schools, relied upon by other attorneys in their briefs.

The Uber arrives and the young lawyer hops into the backseat of the odd-looking car. Not a wreck, merely a dark-green, boxy, generic vehicle without a hint of personality. The driver turns to him — a woman old enough to be his grandmother — smiles and winks. The gig economy has opened up opportunities for everyone, he thinks, even for older folks on fixed incomes. He smiles back and fastens his seatbelt in time for the woman to screech away from the government building.

The young lawyer snaps open his briefcase — a graduation gift from his father, a man who never finished high school but who worked several jobs to make certain his only child could go to college and then law school, something the man and his late wife never could have imagined when they surreptitiously crossed the border into the United States 28 years ago. A young, brave couple who wanted to make a better life for themselves and their soon-to-be-born child in this land of opportunity. Such a shame the man's wife would not survive a brazen, selfish cancer that took her away before their son graduated from law school three years ago.

As the young lawyer riffles through his briefcase, he notices the car has stopped. He looks up and sees brick walls on either side of him. An alley. The woman turns to him, winks, and holds up a finger as if to say: One moment, please. She pops the trunk, hops out, and scurries to the back of the car. The young lawyer shrugs; he has plenty of time before his flight, and resumes his riffling.

After a few minutes, the young lawyer starts to perspire. The woman probably did not leave the air conditioning on as she searched for God-knows-what in her trunk. But wait: The young lawyer hears the car's vents going full blast, but it's hot air, not cold, pouring out. He sighs, snaps shut his briefcase, and reaches for the door handle. He pulls, but nothing happens. He tries again. And again nothing. He scooches over the unusually hard plastic seat to the other door and tries that one, but no success. The young lawyer looks for the door lock but sees smooth plastic where a latch should be. It is getting unbearably hot. He loosens his tie just as the woman slams shut the trunk.

The young lawyer's breathing becomes labored. He turns to search for the woman. She is behind the car, looking at the young lawyer, sharpening a glistening carving knife on a black, rectangular stone. She licks her lips, smiles, winks.

Just as the young lawyer begins to lose consciousness, his mind drifts back to his first day of kindergarten. His beautiful mother walks him up to the school's gate, his little, sweaty hand in hers. She squats, her perfume fills the air with love, and touches her anxious son's cheek. *Mi cielo*, she coos, I love you. Do well and be good. Make us proud.

❖

THE ACTOR

MARIANO ZARO

Once in a while, he comes to see me in the dorm.
He comes unannounced. He sits on top of my desk
with his back against the window.
Can I smoke? he asks. I sit on the bed.
It's a small bed, not comfortable.
I had to put a wood plank under the mattress;
it was too soft. I couldn't sleep.
I still cannot sleep; but it's not because of the mattress.

In the room there is a humble sink, a small mirror,
a glass shelf attached to the wall with rusty brackets.
On the shelf: Toothpaste, shaving cream,
nail clippers. There is also a small plant,
a succulent that my sister gave me the day I left home.
This plant is indestructible, she told me.
But I know that it will die with me in this room;
like many other things.

I have dropped all my classes, he says.
I want to be an actor.
The sun hits his hair, and the hair is wheat,
flames, summer.
He opens the window, lights a cigarette;
keeps the hand outside.

I am going to the Avignon Theater Festival.
Would you like to come? he asks.
I don't know what to say. Avignon is far away.
I have no money. Avignon is for other people.

He turns toward the window,
looks at his reflection in the glass
and messes up his hair.
His profile is less impeccable now, less insulting.

It's getting dark. Under his thin cotton sweater,
his bony shoulders become harder, menacing.
There is no beauty without danger, they say.

He crosses his legs, knees almost touching
the Latin dictionary, my class notes,
and my journal where his name appears
in the same sentence, woven with other words –
grass, impossible, blond, balsamic, *azul*, and magnolia.

LAIDA LEXERTUNDI, FILM STILL FROM *WE HAD THE EXPERIENCE BUT MISSED THE MEANING*, 2014, 16MM, 8 MIN

LOOKING AT THE OCEAN

AMINA CAIN

IN ELENA FERRANTE'S *The Lost Daughter*, the novel's protagonist, Leda, goes alone to the sea on her summer vacation. While there, she thinks of her daughters, far away now in Toronto with their father, and she doesn't miss them. Instead, she becomes focused on another family she sees every day at the beach, especially on a young woman at the center of that family named Nina. Without them knowing, Leda intrudes on the family; she intensifies their drama. For a time, she becomes a confidante to the young woman, giving her advice that is dark but also direct, intimate. At one point, Leda says to Nina: "Sometimes you have to escape in order not to die."

The ocean is many things, of course, but one of them is a screen, something we watch from the beach while absentmindedly projecting our thoughts upon it. Or we read a book, and when we look out at the horizon the book is projected there, too. When we swim, we stay fairly close to the shore. Farther out and the projection grows thinner. We project on to something, on top of it, not *in* it. When Leda is in front of the sea, it is her own life, rather than her absent family, that is projected on top of it; her flawed, complicated self.

In Joanna Walsh's "Vagues" from her book *Vertigo*, a narrator sits in an oyster restaurant with a man who is not her husband, though her husband is projected into the scene, too, in the way she thinks of him. We see also the objects in the restaurant and the other people, the beach and the water, for the story is especially cinematic. The narrator (facing away from the ocean) sits across from the man who is not her husband and thinks:

> Now he is here, seated at the table that looks out at the sea. It is the table he indicated, the table he desired, from which he can see the sea the beach the seagulls the stork the mother the stones the toddler the seaweed the rubbish, and at the other side of the table interrupting his view of all these things, me.

Another vacation, now on the Costa Brava in Roberto Bolaño's *The Third Reich*, begins like this: "Through the window comes the murmur of the sea mingled with the laughter of the night's last revelers, a sound that might be the waiters clearing the tables on the terrace, an occasional car driving slowly along the Paseo Marítimo, and a low and unidentifiable hum from the other rooms in the hotel." As *The Third Reich* goes on, there will be a disappearance, mind/war games, and a kind of madness, though this opening sentence is empty and clear. The ocean mixed with other things, but constant. Soon it will be thoroughly visible and the novel will be a projection upon it. ❖

CONTRIBUTORS
FALL 2016

Carmiel Banasky is the author of the novel *The Suicide of Claire Bishop*. Her work has appeared in *Glimmer Train, The Guardian, American Short Fiction, Guernica, The Rumpus,* and on *NPR,* among other places. She earned her MFA from Hunter College and is the recipient of awards and fellowships from Bread Loaf, Ucross, Ragdale, Artist Trust, I-Park, and other foundations. After four years on the road at writing residencies, she now lives in LA.

Cal Bedient was raised in Washington State and educated at the Whitman College Conservatory of Music and the University of Washington, where he earned a PhD. He is the author of several poetry collections, including *The Multiple* (2012), *Days of Unwilling* (2008), *The Violence of the Morning* (2002), and *Candy Necklace* (1997). His critical writing includes *The Yeats Brothers and Modernism's Love of Mobility* (2008), *He Do the Police in Different Voices: The "Waste Land" and Its Protagonist* (1986), *In the Heart's Last Kingdom: Robert Penn Warren's Major Poetry* (1984), *Eight Contemporary Poets* (1974), and *Architects of the Self: George Eliot, D.H. Lawrence, and E.M. Forster* (1972). A founding editor of the New California Poetry Series, Bedient has also coedited *Lana Turner: A Journal of Poetry and Opinion and VOLT*. He is a professor emeritus at UCLA and lives in Santa Monica, California.

Amina Cain is the author of *Creature*, out with Dorothy, a publishing project. She lives in Los Angeles, where she is working on a novel.

Kim Calder studies contemporary American literature at the University of California, Los Angeles. Her work has appeared in *The Los Angeles Review of Books, Unsaid Literary Journal, The Volta,* and *Jacket2*.

Leonard Chang is the author of seven novels, including the recently published *Triplines*, and the internationally acclaimed *Over the Shoulder*. His newest novel, *The Lockpicker*, is scheduled for publication next year. He's also a TV writer/producer working on shows such as NBC's *Awake* and FX's *Justified*, and currently writes for the new FX/John Singleton show *Snowfall*.

Cathy Linh Che is the author of the poetry collection, *Split* (Alice James Books), winner of the Kundiman Poetry Prize, the Norma Farber First Book Award from the Poetry Society of America, and the Best Poetry Book Award from the Association of Asian American Studies.

Kate Durbin is a Los Angeles-based artist and writer. Her books include *E! Entertainment, The Ravenous Audience,* and *ABRA,* which is also an iPad app. She was the 2015 Arts Queensland Poet in Residence.

Piotr Florczyk is a poet, essayist, and translator of Polish poetry. His most recent books are *East & West,* a volume of poems, and *My People & Other Poems* by Wojciech Bonowicz. Florczyk, a doctoral fellow at USC, lives in Mar Vista with his wife and daughter. For more info, please visit: www.piotrflorczyk.com

Libby Flores is a 2008 PEN Center USA Emerging Voices Fellow. Her short fiction has appeared or is forthcoming in *Post Road Magazine, Tin House/The Open Bar, The Rattling Wall, Paper Darts, FLASH: The International Short-Short Story Magazine,* and *Bridge Eight.* She lives in Los Angeles, but will always be a Texan. She can be found at libbyflores.com.

Dorothy Fortenberry is a playwright and screenwriter. She lives with her husband, composer Colin Wambsgans, and kids in Burbank. She worked most recently as a writer and producer on *The Handmaid's Tale* for Hulu. She wishes it were less relevant, too.

Jen George is the author of the short story collection *The Babysitter at Rest,* out with Dorothy, a publishing project. Her work has appeared in *BOMB, Harper's, n+1,* the *White Review,* and other places. She was born and raised in Southern California, and now spends her time between Los Angeles and New York.

Jill Kato is currently a student in the MFA program at the University of California, Irvine. Her work has previously appeared in *The Threepenny Review* and *New Ohio Review.*

Jen Klein lives in Los Angeles with her family. She is a screenwriter and YA author, currently writing for ABC's *Grey's Anatomy*. Her two published books are *Shuffle, Repeat* and *Jillian Cade: (fake) Paranormal Investigator.* Jen has two more YA contemporary romances coming from Random House in 2017 and 2018.

Eriq La Salle is an actor, director, and author, best known for his award-winning portrayal of Dr. Peter Benton on the critically acclaimed medical drama *ER.* As a writer and author, La Salle has received rave reviews for his *Martyr Maker Series. Laws of Annihilation* is the third book in the series. Eriq La Salle lives in Los Angeles, California.

Janice Rhoshalle Littlejohn is a senior editor for *Los Angeles Review of Books*. She is co-author of *Swirling: How to Date, Mate, and Relate Mixing Race, Culture, and Creed* (Atria Books/Simon & Schuster). Janice is currently co-writing and producing an independent feature film, *Lovers in Their Right Mind*. The script was the only U.S. and only English-language submission selected for the 2016 DreamAgo Plume & Pellicule international workshop in Switzerland. Janice is also producing a documentary on women in jazz, *"...But Can She Play?"* A Southern California native, Janice is a Los Angeles Institute for the Humanities fellow.

Attica Locke is a novelist and screenwriter. Her latest novel, *Pleasantville*, is the 2016 winner of the Harper Lee Prize for Legal Fiction. Her first novel, *Black Water Rising*, was nominated for an Edgar Award, an NAACP Image Award, as well as a Los Angeles Times Book Prize, and was short-listed for the Women's Prize for Fiction. Her second book, *The Cutting Season*, was a national bestseller and the winner of the Ernest Gaines Award for Literary Excellence. She is currently a writer and producer on the Fox drama *Empire*. She also serves on the board of the Library Foundation of Los Angeles. A native of Houston, Texas, Attica lives in Los Angeles, with her husband and daughter.

Lynn Melnick is the author of *Landscape with Sex and Violence* (forthcoming in 2017) and *If I Should Say I Have Hope* (2012), both with YesYes Books, and the co-editor of *Please Excuse This Poem: 100 Poets for the Next Generation* (Viking 2015). She serves on the Executive Board of VIDA: Women in Literary Arts.

Carol Muske-Dukes is the author of eight books of poems, four novels, and two collections of essays. Her ninth poetry collection, *Blue Rose*, is forthcoming from Penguin. She is a professor of English/Creative Writing at USC, where she founded the PhD program in CW/Lit. She is former Poet Laureate of California and recipient of many awards and honors.

Andrew Nicholls has written for television since 1976 and has recent fiction in *Black Clock, New World Writing, The Santa Monica Review, Cosmonauts Avenue, The Boiler Journal*, and elsewhere.

Daniel Olivas is the author of seven books, including, most recently, *Things We Do Not Talk About: Exploring Latino/a Literature through Essays and Interviews* (San Diego State University Press, 2014). He is also co-editor of *The Coiled Serpent: Poets Arising from the Cultural Quakes and Shifts of Los Angeles* (Tía Chucha Press, 2016). "Gig Economy" will be featured in his forthcoming collection, *The King of Lighting Fixtures: Stories* (University of Arizona Press, fall 2017).

Michael Lorenzo Porter grew up in and around Mid-City, Los Angeles, where he was raised by his mother and grandmother. His short stories have appeared in *Killing Fields Journal*, and *LAWS Review No. 1*. His short story "In My Head" was adapted for the screen in Germany as *In Meinem Kopf*.

Thelma T. Reyna is the author of *The Heavens Weep for Us and Other Stories*, the poetry chapbooks *Breath & Bone* and *Hearts in Common*, and the full-length poetry collection *Rising, Falling, All of Us*. She was the Poet Laureate of the Altadena Library District in 2014-2016.

Sarah Vap grew up in Missoula, Montana. She is the author of six collections of poetry. Her most recent book, *Viability*, was selected by Mary Jo Bang for the National Poetry Series, and was released by Penguin in 2016. She lives with her family in Venice, CA, and is completing her PhD at the University of Southern California.

Vickie Vértiz is a writer from southeast Los Angeles and a graduate of Williams College and the University of California, Riverside. A new Macondo Fellow, Vickie's writing can also be read in KCET'S *Departures* series on the 710 Freeway Corridor and in *HOY* magazine. Her poetry collection, *Palm Frond with Its Throat Cut*, will be published in the Camino Del Sol Series from the University of Arizona Press in the fall of 2017.

Mariano Zaro is the author of four bilingual books of poetry: *Where From/Desde donde, Poems of Erosion/Poemas de la erosión, The House of Mae Rim/La casa de Mae Rim* and *Tres letras/Three Letters*. His poems are included in the anthologies *Monster Verse* (Random House), *Wide Awake* (Beyond Baroque), *The Coiled Serpent* (Tía Chucha), *Angle of Reflection* (Arctos Press), and in several magazines in Spain, Mexico, and the United States. He is a professor of Spanish at Rio Hondo College (Whittier, CA). More information at www.marianozaro.com